Real Estate Investing For Passive Income

The Ultimate Step By Step Beginner's Guide For Agent To Finding Strategies In Off Market. How To Make & Not Lose Money Starting From Gone Bad Investments.

©Copyright 2019 By Tony Rental

All rights reserved.

This document is geared towards providing exact and reliable information with regards to the topic and issue covered. The publication is sold with the idea that the publisher is not required to render accounting, officially permitted, or otherwise, qualified services. If advice is necessary, legal or professional, a practiced individual in the profession should be ordered.

From a Declaration of Principles which was accepted and approved equally by a Committee of the American Bar Association and a Committee of Publishers and Associations. In no way is it legal to reproduce, duplicate, or transmit any part of this document in either electronic means or in printed format. Recording of this publication is strictly prohibited and any storage of this document is not allowed unless with written permission from the publisher.

All rights reserved. The information provided herein is stated to be truthful and consistent, in that any liability, in terms of inattention or otherwise, by any usage or abuse of any policies, processes, or directions contained within is the solitary and utter responsibility of the recipient reader.

Under no circumstances will any legal responsibility or blame be held against the publisher for any reparation, damages, or monetary loss due to the information herein, either directly or indirectly. Respective authors own all copyrights not held by the publisher.

The information herein is offered for informational purposes solely, and is universal as so. The presentation of the information is without contract or any type of guarantee assurance.

The trademarks that are used are without any consent, and the publication of the trademark is without permission or backing by the trademark owner. All trademarks and brands within this book are for clarifying purposes only and are the owned by the owners themselves, not affiliated with this document

Sommario

Real Estate Investing For Passive Income 1

    Features Of A Profitable Investment Property 77

        Getting the Information 81

    Keys To Successfully Invest In A Real Estate 84

    How To Correctly Value And Analyze Investment Property 91

    Valuing Property – Big Picture Fundamentals 92

    Specific Steps To Value Your Property Correctly 94

    Valuing Property Is Part Science Part Guess Work 98

    How Find Rental Properties 99

        Find Rental Property Through Realtors 101

        Find Rental Property in Print Media 102

        Find Rental Property at Auctions 103

    How To Finance Rental Properties 105

        Financing Rental Property: The Numbers 107

        Financing Rental Property: Location 109

        Financing Rental Property: Tenants 110

        Financing Rental Property: Your Credit 111

    How To Apply (& Get Accepted) For Real Estate Loans 113

    What Is A Real Estate Loan 114

        Hard Money Loans For Real Estate 116

        Real Estate Bridge Loans 117

        Check Your Credit 118

        Perform A Credit Audit 119

        Pay Off Debt 120

        Determine What You Can Afford 121

Gather Work History 122

Assemble Income Information 122

Down Payment 123

Compare Lenders 123

Get Pre-approved, Not Pre-Qualified.. 124

Getting Ready To Close 125

Determine Profit Potential 128

Maintenance 130

General Tips 130

When to Put It on the Market 132

Close With Confidence! 133

Conclusion 133

Introduction

Real estate is one of the most popular and most profitable investments today. It is needless to say that investing in real estate gives you the ability to generate passive income and a consistent cash flow that will lead you to financial freedom.

Through real estate, it is possible to generate cash flow for retirement and you do not need any college degree to get started.

Furthermore, you also do not need to quit your current job. You also get the opportunity to contribute to the community and lives too. A lot of people wish to get started in investing in real estate, but most usually have a lot holding them back. Most usually complain that they do not have a good credit history, or they just recently got a new job or graduated college and they cannot obtain a bank loan. Some have even tried applying for a bank loan to only get disappointed later on when their application process becomes rejected. Apart from where to get funding for their first deal, some are just afraid. They fear they do not sufficient experience or something might go wrong.

This book has been designed to get you started in the real estate investment. You will also find this guide helpful if you have been in real estate but have not been getting desired results. This guide is here to provide you with all you need to get started in the real estate business with little or no investment capital. Those that have never dreamt of investing in real estate will also find this guide to be really helpful after reading through all the benefits of real estate investing.

Basically, property lease is an asset as ancient as land ownership history. A person is going to buy and rent a property to a tenant.

The lender, the owner, is responsible for paying the property's lease, fees, and upkeep.

According to the United States Census Bureau, this country's real estate has steadily grown in value from 1940 to 2006. While a downturn happened during the 2008-2010 subprime mortgage meltdowns, it has now rebounded and overall has risen.

A buyer should know the market where they are looking for properties and recruiting an expert to assist. The most important aspects to consider are property location and market rental rates for investors seeking an income stream from rental properties. As for the area, there are many popular rentals near major schools. If you buy a property close to a state university, for example, students are likely to want to rent it year after year. A profitable rental property also has many other features, and some take time to learn.

In the phase of what seems to be a perfect project, of course, there are blemishes. You could end up with a bad tenant ruining the estate and, worse yet, ending up with no tenant at all. This leaves you with a negative monthly cash flow, which means you may need to scramble to cover your mortgage payments. There is also the question of finding the correct property. You're going to want to hit up an area where vacancy rates are low and choose a place people want to lease.

Use a mortgage calculator to calculate the total cost of the estate with interest once you have located a suitable home in an area where people want to lease. Researching the different types of loans is also worthwhile to achieve a good interest rate for your loan.

There's nothing better than making money while you're sleeping.

Passive income investment helps you to earn financial returns on your behalf with little or no effort — perfect for real estate investors with day jobs or other time commitments.

An ideal form of passive income is rental income. Nonetheless, if you already own at least one rental house— or something more complicated like an apartment building— you are well aware that such assets require any active involvement, such as routine maintenance, rent collection, and lease management.

There are a variety of outlets that allow you to reap the rewards without getting off the sofa if you want to benefit from the good returns to real estate without having to do any work at all.

Here are several choices worth looking into for passive real estate.

Crowdfunding

Real estate investing is exactly what it sounds like: investor parties joining forces to buy commercial properties, apartment complexes, and portfolios of single-family homes.

Mostly managed and run through online platforms, crowdfunding real estate allows you to own a piece of a profitable home building or cluster with just a few taps on the screen.

Example: Online crowdfunding platforms such as Fundrise, PeerStreet, and RealtyMogul provide opportunities for casual investors to join multi-million-dollar real estate ventures. With property purchases, these companies tend to be very selective, thoroughly reviewing them, and providing data and reports to be revealed.

Creating online accounts, transferring their investments, selecting an investment, and seeing their money grow.

Pros:

You can start small: Low minimum investment is needed for many crowdfunding sites.

It's very hands-off: there are no changing light fixtures or mowing lawns.

Easily diversified: crowdfunding minimizes risk by offering multiple asset classes, including multi-family, land, and commercial property.

The flexibility of location: This platform also allows you to improve cash flow by competing in warmer markets.

Cons:

Smaller returns: your profits will not be as high as if you were the owner of a rental property.

Not easy to opt-out: Most real estate crowdfunders need your investment to be frozen in time, making it difficult to cash out at a notice.

More control: Calls are made by fund managers while buying properties, sites, etc.

REITs

Real Estate Investment Trusts (REITs) are like mutual funds invested exclusively in real estate. Unlike crowdfunding, REITs encourage passive investors to engage without the high barrier in major real estate deals. Nevertheless, they vary from investing in that their portfolios include a wide range of properties at once, rather than selecting from individual properties.

Three forms of REITs exist:

- Exchange-traded: registered with the SEC and listed on exchanges such as the NYSE.
- Non-traded: these REITs, although listed with the SEC, do not exchange publicly.
- Private: These are not exchanged on exchanges or reported with the SEC.

Example: REITs may be unique or general. Others invest in cell towers and data centers solely. A traditional REIT could use its assets to purchase large apartment complexes in major cities, creating equity for investors at the same time as handling individual properties and tenants. Investors can buy shares in REITs as simple as buying shares of stocks and funds via regular markets.

Pros:

Less risk: a well-managed REIT mitigates risk by incorporating large property conglomerates rather than individual properties.

Multiple income streams: In addition to long-term appreciation, REITs deliver annual dividend income.

Portfolio diversification: Some real estate investors use REITs as a third investment option after stocks and mutual funds.

Cons:

Market volatility: exchange-linked REITs. It can drag REITs down with it if the NYSE has a bad day.

Higher returns: REITs are expected to share 90% of their annual profits, which is good in the short term but allows less to spend confidence.

No control: Unlike investing, you don't have a tangible asset or the ability to control assets, unlike direct ownership.

Tax Liens

If homeowners do not pay taxes, county governments put a lien on their homes. To recover the lost tax income, the county also auctions creditors who receive interest from them off the tax liens.

Example: When you win an auction for a tax lien, you earn interest until the householder pays the unpaid taxes. When a tax payment is sent to the county by the homeowner, you receive your share and interest accrued.

Pros:

High interest: tax liabilities can yield interest rates above 12% or higher, which means that ownership of a few liabilities could lead to some decent passive income.

Acquiring ownership: although uncommon, bankruptcy can take place if taxes are unpaid for a specified period. In such a case, at a deep discount, the tax lien holder could acquire the deed.

Service of use: often, online tax-link auctions are held, making it relatively easy to join.

Cons:

Due diligence: tax relations entail a limited amount of research— e.g., mortgage records, other home ties — and some states require tax lien holders to periodically alert property owners that they are lien holders.

The burden of foreclosure: although it is tempting to purchase a penny house on the dollar, foreclosures on tax lien are uncommon and difficult.

Not secure enough: keeping a lien on someone else's home might seem too risky for some investors, not to mention a potential worm might.

Remote Ownership

Remote ownership of property is an ideal combination of personal ownership of property and absolute passivity. This is when a property owner uses an online platform like Roofstock for tenants and property management already in place to find, review, and lease from state rental properties.

Many property owners rarely — or never —visit their investment property. They just let the property managers do their work and month after month collects the rent.

Example: A resident of San Francisco wants to build a single-family home portfolio but lacks the funds to do that locally. Remote property platforms provide an opportunity for out-of-state investors to own turnkey rental properties in more affordable markets with more room for appreciation.

The buyer will browse through a range of properties while shopping on eBay, add them to an online cart, make a bid, and close.

Pros:

Lower returns: Like investing and REITs, remote real estate investment offers full property ownership. This means that all the rent (minus costs) and gratitude will go into your account.

Accessible data: For example, Roofstock offers a database with key stats, details, and home information to help investors make smart purchases.

Position Diversification: Remote investment in real estate makes it easier to diversify ownership across multiple areas to reduce the risk of a market downturn.

Cons:

Property distance: some property owners may feel unseen skittish about buying a home sight.

Renter reliability: A diligent application process will root out bad renters, but there is always a risk that one might be late on rent, hard to communicate with, or suddenly move out.

Time to Sell: When it comes to selling, no property owner can predict how long a property will remain on the market. It can be expensive to delay. Nevertheless, most online real estate companies make it easy to sell your property back to customers who want tenants in place across their programs, which ensures that while waiting for the sale, you can continue earning income.

Money Lending

Do you have the money for a plan to restore and sell, but not the patience for all the work involved? Lending hard money is another reactive path for real estate. In such cases, you can hold the note — or fund the down payment — for someone else's fully controlled renovation / fast-selling plan.

Example: Expert repair and flippers often juggle multiple projects at once. We will resort to hard money loans to help them fund the cost if we find a great deal without the ability to borrow more. Often these loans are shorter-term and cheaper than conventional loans.

Pros:

100% Passive Investment: You are participating in a labor-intensive real estate venture with no finger raising.

More money: cash-strapped remodelers borrow at a higher interest rate, which means bigger investment returns.

Quicker turnaround: you could get your money back quicker, given that these works mostly wrap up within a year.

Cons:

More power: Unless you have specific contractual terms, someone else will be in charge of the repairs, upgrades, and development.

Higher risk: It can go awry even the best-laid fix and flips. If the plan loses money or defaults on the creditor, it is a lost cause.

Rules and regulations: the rules governing hard money lending of real estate vary from state to state. You will need to test them out in advance.

Factors To Consider Before Saying "Yes" To A Passive Commercial Real Estate Deal

- Who's your sponsor?
- What is the basis?
- What's the market like?

Commercial Investment Sponsor

If reviewing a commercial real estate contract, one of the first things you need to remember is who the investor is. Also known as owners or investors, supporters are the individuals (usually a corporation or a commercial real estate company) who is determined to help you buy or grow the contract. Most specifically, it is the lender who will serve as a fiduciary in your contract; they are the ones who are tasked with helping you to complete the deal. You might even argue that in a given commercial commodity, sponsors simultaneously maximize the payoff and mitigate the risk. Therefore, partnering with a successful partner is in the best interest; this way, you can increase your chances of success.

Commercial Basis Metric

Another way to report the "all-in" value per square foot of the target property is the economic base measure. Nonetheless, the definition is often used more precisely to compare two similar properties. An appealing base is a great indicator of how you can expect a property to work compared to neighboring comparables. If you can equate the foundation of your estate with a comparable asset that is already being utilized, you can gauge how well yours is going to perform.

Best Commercial Market

We've always read about the golden rule of property: location. Wherever you spend, the value of your property plays an integral role, and commercial property is no exception. Note due diligence to determine the best possible market for your purposes is in the best interest. The economy needs to support your target if you intend to invest in commercial real estate. In other words, if you're buying commercial real estate, make sure there's a continuing market for it.

Passive capital is part of the portfolio of an owner, so the commercial property is no exception. While the entrance hurdle is higher than that of single-family homes, those who can invest effectively in passive commercial real estate should find the rewards worth the hard work. After all, one of the best long-term exit strategies out there is passive income through commercial real estate. When you know how to invest in commercial real estate, you may want to explore sooner rather than later adding it to your portfolio.

Benefits of Real Estate Investing

One of the benefits of real estate investment is that it gives you a unique ability to build equity. Equity is a commodity that belongs to your net worth. You build equity as you pay off your mortgage. You now have the leverage to acquire additional rental properties as you build equity and increase your cash flow.

You get the ability to generate a passive income that is almost tax-free by investing in real estate. Your rental properties are going to work in your sleep for you, and you have nothing to worry about. By buying several rental properties that generate sufficient income to cover your expenses, you have the freedom to do what you enjoy, rather than spending your entire time at work.

Investing in real estate is a stable way to increase wealth over some time when done correctly. One of the many advantages of real estate investment is that it can provide retirement cash flow. It means it can bring revenue from your rental properties to your retirement years.

While most investors concentrate on ROI, CAP, cash flow, and other financial metrics, the effect on the environment is an immense and unquantified advantage for investing in real estate. Responsible real estate investors are improving the communities by improving the housing available, maintaining properties, and increasing local tax revenues. It affects the neighborhoods positively and improves the lives of those who live there. By acquiring and restoring a dilapidated house, one not only eliminates an eyesore but also increases the self-esteem of residents living around the home. The mom-and-pop real estate investors are a bright spot in a world where developers are synonymous with unregulated speculation which affects things for the better.

There are many ways to invest and become an entrepreneur in real estate. For a profit, you can buy a home, fix it, and put it back on the market. Buy a property to hold and create wealth for the appreciation. You might become a landlord and begin buying rental homes, multi-family homes, or even apartments. Perhaps the development of land is for you. You're the owner.

Investing in real estate offers protection from depreciation, as well as the advantages of having a physical asset in the diversification of portfolios. Real estate is a tangible asset that can always be monetized, regardless of financial market conditions, by renting or residing in the property. Compared to traditional stocks or bonds, it makes it much more robust to capital market swings. Real estate is part of the broader alternative investment category that encompasses everything from art to collectibles and physical gold. The tangibility of real estate also provides a sense of stability to property owners during bear markets or short-term stock sales.

While most people are afraid of inflation, in real estate investors, this is not the case. An excellent hedge against inflation is investment in properties. As the price level rises, so does the property's rental income and the valuation of your savings. This ensures that both the immediate and long-term effects of inflation benefit real estate investors. While this may not be the first advantage of investing in real estate, which comes to mind, it should be taken into account because an increase in the cost of living is correlated with a rise in their cash flow to real estate investors. Throughout recent decades, the average annual real estate appreciation rate across the world has been roughly 6 percent, while the inflation rate rarely approaches 4 percent.

There are various reasons for investing in real estate. It is a proven way of building wealth over time, and when leased, it can help generate cash. It can also provide you with depreciation tax benefits, and this can help to increase your returns.

Investing in real estate can be an alternative to a savings tool. Young families are encouraged to invest in purchasing one property for each child they think is going to attend university. It allows families to save through the payments of the renters. You can either sell or continue to use the property as a means of cash flow when the asset is paid off.

At least one house or a piece of property should be owned by everyone. The ability to generate wealth by growth, building capital, and hedging against inflation is one of the many advantages of investing in real estate. It can also provide passive rental property income with cash flow. These are the reasons that the investment portfolio should include real estate as a key component.

By comparison with investing in the stock market, interest in real estate does not fluctuate wildly daily. It's a stable asset that gives you an income. You are merely regularly earning your continuing profit (known as Money on Cash Return) and hoping to sell when the price is high, and the demand is high. The demand in every area, of course, is not the same, and incentives for buying and selling will vary considerably across the world. Some people compare investment in real estate to investment in shares because real estate provides the investor with steady cash flow. Bonds, however, are more prone to volatility in the economy. Real estate properties will not change the price automatically on the grounds of equity investments or due to political uncertainty. This makes a secure and stable investment in real estate. In many cases, property investments also offer the owners attractive tax advantages.

Real estate is easy to fund as an investment vehicle for the property. At attractive rates, you can borrow 50 to 90 percent of the acquisition cost, often rates below the anticipated annual return on investment. Positive leveraging is also the ability to magnify the investment return with financing. When used as collateral for finance, shares, bonds, services, and art do not provide the same convenience.

For many individuals and institutional investors, industrial real estate has been a very attractive investment. Recently, there has been a major increase in the amount of money pursuing commercial real estate possession. For two factors, prices are rising. The first is that rental rates continue to rise due to the demand for these facilities and the rising cost of construction. Second, as the number of investors bidding on commercial real estate investments tends to reduce the cap level or yield, this is increasing prices.

Real estate will outsource classic investing as you don't have to spend in the entire investment sum. If you were going to invest $200,000 in the stock market, you would have to put $200,000 in total. You could do that with as little as $40,000 out-of-pocket if you wanted to invest in a duplex for $200,000. For the loan, the bank puts up 80% of the money, but you get 100% of the income. If both increased at the same level, the return on the investment in real estate would be significantly higher because you only put up 20% of the investment scenario.

One overlooked the benefit of investment in real estate, particularly residential real estate, is the pride in helping others to provide a home. Everyone needs a roof over their heads, but not everyone has the resources upfront to buy a home, making renting them the only other option. We often hear of landlords shirking their responsibilities and for some tenants making living conditions straight nightmarish. Not only do you help a family house by investing in a residential property, but you also ensure that the family is housed in safe, healthy, clean and fair conditions.

One of the advantages of growth in real estate is the opportunity to help the local economy. As an investor in real estate, you will have the opportunity to employ licensed local contractors, buy building materials, and generally stimulate the local economy near the building site.

If you own multiple properties, you may be able to change your primary residence from one residence to another if you decide to do so later in your life. Many people prefer a two-story house when they raise a family, but in their golden years, they decide to downsize to a one-story because it is easier for them to manage.

Mitigating risk is one of the biggest benefits of having real estate in one's investment portfolio. Of course, having a monthly calculated income is an outstanding benefit, but it is often important to have insulation against higher-risk investments such as stocks. Having the right balance of immovable property in one's portfolio will provide just enough diversification to help offset risk by not focusing on a single investment profile.

Section 1031 of the Internal Revenue Code allows you to delay paying your property's sale tax once you spend the profits in another estate. This is because the IRS thinks you're planning to swap your old property for another asset. Nevertheless, the new property, of equal or greater value, should be of the same sort like the old property. You should also find the new property and include it in the official documents within 45 days of selling the old property, and you have to close the deal within 180 days. In order to qualify for the 1031 Registry, you will also need an agent to manage the payments.

Investing in real estate gives investors a wide range of opportunities, according to Bankable Insight. Depending on your initial startup capital, leverage, and personal preference, you have the option to invest in single-family residences, multi-family homes, vacant land, and commercial buildings. Even if you don't have enough real estate investment expertise, once you have the money or capital to buy a property, you can still get going.

Aside from the fact that most real estate values are usually appreciated, even during a difficult time, your real estate investment can never go down to zero. Morris Invest claims that when you own one, you can always sell your other. Immobility, unlike stock, never b

5 Reasons to Consider Passive Income Investing

The ideas of real estate investment and passive income were conflated by many individuals. Immovable property can be a form of passive capital, but often not in the way investors think. Passive investing in real estate can be one of the most powerful ways to get your money to work for you. But before we address the specific benefits of passive investment in real estate, we need to illustrate what this type of investment is — and as critically explain how and why it is distinct from active investment in real estate.

Most people imagine owning and leasing a piece of residential property, such as a single-family home, condominium unit, or apartment complex, as a passive investment in real estate. We see this as passive income because they buy a piece of land, rent it out, and then receive payments from the renters each month while they visualize the investment played out. But it's not a passive investment in real estate.

At a minimum, the buyer must pick the properties to buy in this case and then consult with a property management company and make regular choices on issues such as what tenants to take, whether to repair or remove a broken water heater and when to re-carpet or paint the house. If the investor chooses not to outsource these operational tasks to a property management company, they will have to manage daily property ownership responsibilities themselves. This is a successful purchase of the real estate.

So, what do we mean by passive income, and what investments are passive real estate?

What Is A Passive Income Investment?

Passive revenue typically refers to a somewhat automatic income stream. You make an upfront investment in money— often in a bond or mutual fund or another equity-based asset— and then obtain an ownership interest in that portfolio from which you receive dividends or other forms of regular income.

That makes this form of profit passive is that you don't control the money directly.

What Is Passive Real Estate Investing?

Therefore, passive real estate investment is a type of real estate investment in which you put your money in a real estate project that is not going to have any direct management obligation.

You can invest actively in real estate in several ways— such as buying stock in publicly traded real estate-related businesses. These may include property development agencies, major real estate brokers, or construction firms. You can also invest in Real

Estate Investment Trusts (REITs), which are companies that pool the assets of investors to participate in large property transactions.

And due to the emergence of real estate investing, you can now also make direct investments in single real estate deals— pooling your money in equity or debt-based assets with other investors— while still retaining all the potential benefits of passive real estate investment.

If you invest in real estate through a crowdfunding platform, you can find deals, usually debt-based loans, that can give you a fixed monthly fee over a set period of time. You can also consider investment opportunities on a crowdfunding platform which allows you to take an equity stake in the transaction, where you can take part in the continuing profits and/or the property's overall gain, and reap these potential rewards when the money is dispersed.

With several targets, you can actively invest in real estate. For example, you can invest in passive income— paid out in a debt-based portfolio as either daily dividend in an equity investment, or as fixed payments (with interest). Or you can save actively for development in real estate— in other words, the investment property value and gain until resold. You can also invest in a passive real estate for both the ongoing profit as well as the potential for longer-term growth.

Depending on the incentives we can discuss below, if you are searching for a passive income source, real estate can be one of the better passive investment vehicles available. What is important to understand now is that incremental investing in real estate can be a great way to add to your residual income.

What Is Residual Income?

Residual income applies to the revenue that exists for an individual or business after all liabilities and costs have been charged, typically measured annually.

How Can I Generate Additional Residual Income?

Establishing investments in passive income can be an efficient way of generating extra residual income. You put your assets in a debt-or equity-structured portfolio— shares, real estate, etc. — and take advantage of that investment's regular income flow. Because you only make this contribution annually, these regular payments are added to your residual income directly.

Reasons Passive Income Investing Might Be For You

You'll Have Someone Working for You

Passive real estate allows tax-delayed cash returns in an equity-structured investment that can allow you to keep more of your earnings.

This is one reason we said earlier that immovable property could be a more powerful passive investment than other forms of passive investment. Unlike interest payments or stock dividends that can be taxed at your highest income bracket, the pass-through potential property ownership benefit allows you to offset your income by your share of the depreciation expense.

You Won't Have to Deal with Tenants, Toilets or Trash

When you're a conservative real estate investor, you're not familiar with the everyday management problems directly. Around 2 am, you won't get a message. Broken door? Calling the handyman is not your responsibility.

You Won't Have to Deal with a Bank

It is difficult to work with lenders to secure financing. Because the economy has gone south, lenders have started to demand even more paperwork to receive loans, and the process is time-consuming as well as mind engaging.

When you are a passive investor in real estate, your portfolio is linked to a qualified private real estate investment company that already has partnerships with select banks. In your name, they manage the waters of bank financing, so you don't have to.

Your Passive Investment Lets You Leverage the Expertise and Experience of Others

Whether that means trading in shares through an online brokerage or owning your investment property, you always have the choice in any investment to go it alone. But to harness the intelligence of the people around you, there's something to admit.

Many real estate investors devote their lives to understanding the business in and out, and passive investing in real estate allows you to take advantage of their intense knowledge.

You Can Make Money While You Sleep

Passive investment in real estate can be fast. You are doing your due diligence, signing electronic legal paperwork, and almost instantly transferring money. And as soon as the transaction is collected, you become an investor in that real estate company and may begin to realize a passive income or a part of the development of that venture.

In other words, while you sleep, you have the potential to make money. Your money works for you 24/7, primarily when you invest in properties with existing tenants where cash flow exists.

What Are Some Additional Passive Income Ideas?

You can research publicly traded real estate companies and public real estate investment trusts (REITs) if you are looking for other ways to invest passively in real estate. You may also want to investigate private REITs that are not traded on any stock exchange publicly. However, be aware that private REITs are not also subject to the same rules on financial disclosure as public REITs or other publicly traded businesses.

If you are interested in passive investment opportunities other than real estate, you can also explore the many ways you can invest in traditional stocks, bonds, and mutual funds. With the convenience of opening an online trading account and the historically low cost of buying and selling the issues, making passive equity market portfolios is easier and cheaper than ever before.

Nevertheless, it is important to remember that the interest you receive on stock dividends can be paid at your daily income's highest level. Nevertheless, a passive interest of real estate— such as a share in a portfolio of assets you buy through a real estate investing agency — allows you to gain tax benefits that function to mitigate your regular income.

What Are The Risks Of Passive Income Investing?

Basically, investment in real estate also carries risks, as does investment in any asset class. You carry the ongoing risk of your principal's loss when you invest in any passive income asset. In the case of both stock or a REIT investment, this can result when the value of the investment goes down— either because of internal problems with the underlying asset (the company whose shares you purchased, or the REIT real estate portfolio) or because of a general market downturn. In either case, the asset's value can decrease.

That's why it's so important that you first have to do your research before you make any investment— whether in real estate or some other asset class, active or passive. Any investment will promise that all of the capital will return or even cover you. But your due diligence can help you find for your capital safer and perhaps more lucrative investments.

Choosing The Right Real Estate Exit Strategy

The truly ambitious, especially in the residential redevelopment field, acknowledges the importance of an efficient business model. Establishing an established system, a strategy if you like, has the potential to push any company to the forefront of their respective industry. Consequently, in the presence of a well-designed strategy, both monetary benefits and personal development can increase exponentially. Therefore, the value of an exit strategy for real estate should never be ignored.

Those who take the time to get familiar with each procedure's intricacies can be rewarded accordingly. In comparison, those who fail to recognize the value of an effective exit strategy for real estate may be deprived of the opportunity to achieve prominence in their business. In Alan Lakein's terms, "Failing to plan is planning to fail." Essentially, assessing their success relative to their competitors is up to the individual shareholder. Implementing one of several well-designed exit strategies for real estate will certainly give anybody a significant advantage over their competitors.

What Is A Business Exit Strategy?

A strategy for leaving a business is the intention of an investor to either sell or transfer ownership in a company. Just what it looks like is an exit strategy: a way out. It can be used by business owners either to make a profit or to reduce losses if necessary. Usually, business owners dream about possible exit strategies before ever starting a business. This is because exit plans not only to provide a way out of the organization; they also help to drive management decisions along the way.

When it comes to planning a company's exit strategy, there is no one correct answer. Many business owners will choose to sell shares to a mutual partner, while others may expect at some point in time to close the business. The optimal exit depends on the size of the organization, the schedule and financial goals of the holders, and more. Suffice it to say: it takes careful consideration to choose the right business exit strategy. Nonetheless, it can act as an end goal and motivator for business owners when properly planned.

What Is A Real Estate Exit Strategy?

Real estate exit strategies are projects in which the buyer is planning to withdraw from a real estate deal. The decision to implement a successful exit strategy is critical to success, as the right approach would ensure maximum revenue and minimum risks.

All too often, investors fail to realize the importance of learning about effective exit strategies for real estate. As a result, we took the time to provide a roadmap to several exit strategies for like-minded individuals.

Why Is Having An Exit Strategy Important?

An exit strategy is important because it not only controls the actions of an investor throughout a given transaction but also determines how the productivity will be maximized. While speed of implementation is paramount when attempting to facilitate a transaction, do not attempt to initiate an agreement without evaluating potential exit strategies. As an investor, assessing each scenario with the end in mind is critical. That is, once you purchase it, have a specific plan for each building. Before they even encounter a potential developer, buyers should have a clear understanding of how they plan to benefit from any real estate investment.

Familiarizing with each person exit strategy can save your company thousands of dollars, if not millions, over your entire career. It's never prudent to negotiate knowingly with a dealer without understanding how you're going to exit the offer. Blind arrogance will not only raise risks, but it will also eviscerate any potential opportunity from a position of power to compromise. Neglecting to find an exit strategy reduces potential profits while rising risks at the same time.

How To Choose The Right Exit Strategy

The decision on which strategies to use real estate investment is not as rudimentary as it might seem. While planning an exit strategy, there are several main factors to consider. Every deal's future productivity is associated with the preferred approach.

Understanding each plan will help each investor maximize their investment returns.

Sadly, in specific scenarios, there is no golden rule that differentiates between each technique. Knowing which property exit strategy to use, therefore depends on the familiarity of the investor with the following factors:

- Short and long-term goals
- Level
- Time to close
- Purchase price
- Terms
- Property value
- Condition of the property
- Market conditions
- Supply and demand
- Location of the property

Learning each of these individual factors will ultimately decide which of the approaches an investor will follow for exiting real estate.

Top 7 Real Estate Strategies

- Wholesaling
- Flipping
- Buy And Hold Real Estate

- Seller Financing
- Lease Options
- Prehabbing
- Bank Owned Homes
- Traditional

Strategies for leaving real estate are directly correlated with the person operating on them. Based on their desired outcome, investors are required to delineate between each option. The exit strategy that they choose depends on how much money they want to spend in the company and how much experience they have. It is important to note that there is no approach that is right or wrong. Learning all the different ways to get out of a bargain, though, will improve productivity, as you will be able to navigate even the most ambiguous contracts. Below is a comprehensive list of approaches to be taken into account in the future:

Wholesaling

The shareholder will be observed by a sales transaction as the broker between a seller and an end purchaser. Essentially, for a reasonable profit margin, the buyer can locate and sell a property easily. There are two options a purchaser will wholesale: they can either sell or "assign" their purchase contract to an end-user, or they actually close the property and then resell the product to another investor in the case of a "double closing." Wholesalers usually do not spend personal capital on promoting sales and will charge a wholesale price. Such factors make wholesale an appealing way to start investing in real estate

Flipping

Rehabbing, more commonly referred to as house flipping, provides the largest profit margins as it encourages an owner to sell the desired home at full market value. A renovation involves buying, renovating, and selling a house for more than the original cost of construction (purchase price and cost of repair). The recipe for a good flip deal includes locating a property in a market where demand is solid, creating a stable group of contractors, adhering to the renovation schedule and timetable, and eventually selling the property to the highest possible bid quickly. Since there are different factors that can go wrong, though, flipping has some associated risk to remember. For more detail, see our rehabbing checklist to learn how the pros do it.

Buy And Hold Real Estate

Buying and holding property is a concept similar to rehabbing. Nonetheless, a developer wants to rent it out to earn monthly cash flow instead of selling the renovated house. This option is different from simply buying a property at market value and making it a rental property due to the rehabbing added as an extra step. Buying a property at a great price and then improving its reliability and attractiveness with some maintenance and upgrades will not only raise the value of the property (and therefore the return on your investment), it will also allow you to increase rental rates. This is a popular exit strategy for those seeking to build an asset's equity. Nonetheless, make sure you are ready to accept property management obligations.

Seller Financing

The Seller Financing Strategy, as its name suggests, involves an innovative technique that allows the lender to sell the property to the buyer. The investor is investing the transaction and functioning as a lender. Nonetheless, the manager collects monthly payments. To cover the selling price, the lender retains the mortgage loan. This type of arrangement gives the buyer and the seller more flexibility than financing through a lender. When you buy property, seller funding will allow you to buy more properties, will not affect your credit score, and will provide a faster closing process. However, you may be able to negotiate to put down for a down payment little to no down. Allowing customers to fund the order from you as the dealer makes the business listings stand out. Seller financing can also create a pool of monthly income—likely at a high-interest rate—and also distribute tax requirements.

Lease Options

A lease option, better known as the rent-to-own option, requires the holder to rent the house to a borrower, but with the option of buying it later. Usually, a lease agreement will be negotiated between the landlord and the occupant, after which the homeowner will have the option to buy the property from the owner. Once the rental period is over, and the owner wants to continue with the acquisition, their monthly payments will then be made for the property's purchase. Such fees will not be the same as paying mortgage payments, but instead of a creditor, they will be paid to the owner.

Prehabbing

Prehabbing is both a rehabbing and wholesaling type form. Less work is done during a pre-habilitation to get the property up to sale value, making it a great choice for buyers who are interested in doing a bit of "DIY," without the full commitment needed in a fix-and-flip house. Examples of ways to rehabilitate include giving a home a new paint job inside and outside, updating the landscaping, and possibly replacing the carpet. Perhaps need not be overly expensive or difficult and are usually limited to tasks that can be done without a professional's assistance. Nonetheless, it is entirely up to the consumer to spend the amount of time, energy and money spent in a prehab. These are often sold to rehabbers who are going to keep repairing it.

Bank Owned Homes

A property owned by a bank or real estate owned (REO) is a property sold by a lending institution, like a bank. When a property has been foreclosed, it will be taken back into its possession by the financing entity and sold to a new buyer under market value. Because holding and maintaining these properties is expensive for banks, selling them as soon as possible is in their best interest. Typically, they will remove any outstanding liabilities and debts from the property to do so. Bank-owned homes are sold through real estate auctions or sold through the special REO listing website of the lender. Learning how to navigate the real estate auction process, while not your standard exit strategy, may result in some great deals learning how to navigate real estate auctions.

Traditional

A traditional exit strategy is essential to buy a property and then negotiate with a broker to sell it at a higher price. Usually, lenders who rely on this approach would finance the property themselves or deal with a developer for mortgages. Because of its flexibility, a conventional exit strategy is attractive; however, investors who do not buy on the right market can face high holding costs and small profit margins. The viability of a buy and sell transaction depends entirely on the home's purchase price; it will only be possible to resell the house for so much without a full recovery buyer. Therefore, investors need to ensure that they secure the best possible buying price to

Steps to Get Started (or Restarted)

The steps below show you how to start investing in real estate. I recommend that you go through them from start to finish for the best effect.

Identify Your Financial Stage

Investing in real estate is just a vehicle for improving your finances. Now, let's talk about your overall financial image before we get into the specifics of real estate.

Eventually, most new investors want to achieve financial independence. You can conceive of this as the mountain peak where all of the living expenses are paid by investment income.

Whether you trade in real estate or anything else, the fundamentals of scaling this mountain are the same. You need to increase the savings rate to reach the peak of the mountain sooner. Instead, like real estate, you will spend such savings on your preferred property.

Choose a Specific Real Estate Investing Strategy

You should build a 30-page business plan that would be proud of even an MBA at this point. Yet note, the only goal is to get going. So let's start with faster stuff. If you want, you will later create a large, detailed plan.

Pick ONE real estate strategy to help you transition from your current financial level to the next stage.

Starting with a specific strategy doesn't guarantee that later you won't have any detours or even a total change of direction. Life is going on, and you've got to be flexible. But it will help you focus on starting with just one. And that will give you the confidence to get going.

Pick a Target Market

In many places, with costs so high, people often ask me if they should spend close to home or choose a new market. It's a good question because, in the final results, the area you choose can make a big difference.

I prefer to be able to invest close to home IF. Being local gives you the advantage of having intimate market knowledge. And while it is possible to manage real estate from a distance, being local is even more efficient and effective.

So, I'd continue analyzing near-home markets. In your local neighborhoods, if prices seem too high, first explore some ideas locally before looking at other locations. First, drive away for an hour. The suburbs of major urban areas often become much more affordable and reasonable investment. Third, look at your overall market for smaller niches. Niches such as condos, mobile homes, tax liabilities, and invest in the note can still sometimes be profitable within high-priced markets.

But whether you're staying close to home or investing elsewhere, market analysis should always be done first.

Build Your Team

Real estate is a teamwork, and you're your team's leader. You don't necessarily need employees, but you'll need independent contractors and consultants who can assist you in their expertise areas. When you shut off the idea of running this project, then maybe another type of investment would suit you better.

Line Up Financing

Unlike other forms of investment, using the funding to help you with a real estate purchase is quite normal. And there are plenty of choices to make.

The seven sources of funding include:

- Loans from FHA (Federal Housing Administration)– Federal government approved and cheaper than most loans to apply for. The terms include a small down

payment, a fixed rate of interest and a long-term (long) mortgage
- Loans from VA (Veterans Administration)—You must be a qualified veteran. Terms include a down payment of 0 percent, a fixed interest rate, and a long-term loan.
- Banks enforcement—Loans conform with Fannie Mae and Freddie Mac's lending giant rules. A 5%–20% down payment, a fixed interest rate, and a long-term loan may be included in the terms.
- Portfolio Loans—Instead of being paid off on the mortgage market, these are owned by banks or lending institutions. Terms differ, but they typically have a shorter term (5-10 years) and competitive interest rates.
- Hard Money Loans—Instead of detailed borrowing laws from other outlets, these borrowers are most interested in equity (i.e., hard assets). The value of the mortgage is much higher, and they are often used for short-term repairs.
- Private Lenders —Private lenders vary widely, ranging from self-directed IRAs & 401ks to rich individuals. They are extremely valuable because of the flexibility and the long-term relationship you get from these lenders.
- Seller Financing—This is my favorite financing form. A shareholder can allow you to pay the purchase price with installments over time or use more creative contracts such as leases and options. Getting dealer funding is not

as easy as walking into a store, but the versatility of terms makes it worth the effort to fund sellers.

Raise Cash For Your Down Payment & Reserves

Investing in real estate is a business that enables you to use the money of other people to help you move forward. But with no money down, you should not count on building your entire business. Even if you use the lowest interest examples, such as 0 percent down on VA (Veterans Administration) mortgages, you're always going to want to save reserve funds.

Okay, how much money are you going to need? And how are you bringing it up?

Your strategy, the prices on your target market, and your property criteria will depend on how much cash you need. You can also ask your member of the lending team how much down payment you will need for some loan programs.

Let's assume, for example, that your financial goal is to raise your savings rate. You decide to purchase a duplex for $150,000 using the house hacking strategy. You may be able to find a 3.5% down payment FHA mortgage. Okay, for your down payment, you'll need $5,250 (3% of $150,000) and maybe another $3,000 for your closing costs. But for property improvements and reserves for a rainy day, you may also need more cash. Okay, let's say that you need another $10,000.

Marketing Budget

If you have a marketing budget of $0.00, you need to be innovative and instead plan to spend more personal time. That way, it is more difficult, but it is not impossible. You currently have enough to create workable marketing campaigns at about $500 a month. And you can differentiate yourself within the market for $1,000 a month or more.

Marketing investment has always been one of my best returns as an entrepreneur on investment. But with the right marketing strategies, you have to choose your bucks carefully.

Marketing Campaigns

There are plenty of marketing campaigns to choose from. And because advertising is an inconsistent process, strategies like the wind are evolving successfully. So, I recommend that you test various campaigns carefully, and then stick to what works.

Here is a list of my brief explanations of some of the most effective campaigns. They are arranged according to the cost:

Free & Low Cost:

MLS Promotion–Choose the agent of a purchaser to give you leads based on your requirements. Such brokers will set up automatic notifications using the MLS (multiple listing service) that will enter your mailbox whenever a new or diminished property hits the market. Alert—move quickly (like this minute, not hours or days) on these deals! This campaign is also being done by everyone else.

Referral & Networking Promotion—Give links to prospective assets to everyone you meet. Talk to friends and family, but also reach professional contacts such as your CPA, lawyer, financial consultants, real estate agents, property managers, etc. Attend networking sessions at associations of landlords, REIAs (Real Estate Investment Associations), and other conferences related to real estate and industry. Order business cards and print posters to remind people of you with your investing qualifications.

Drive (or cycle) for dollars—walk or drive your streets regularly. Look for signs from FSBO (For Sale By Owner), signs from For Rent, empty or run-down properties identified by brokers, and vacant properties without signs. Dial numbers on signage were possible to communicate to owners or staff. If possible, talk to the neighbors to try to get in touch with the owner for vacant properties. Write down the abandoned address of the house and then look up the contact information of the owner later. Using your local online tax assessor files, you can locate the mailing address, and sometimes you can find phone numbers use whitepages.com or similar online directory lists. You can either call them in the mail or send them a letter asking them to buy their house.

Find Wholesalers & "Bird Dogs" –Some people find deals for other investors. Usually, wholesalers purchase (or control) offers and then market them easily to other shareholders like you for a slight markup. Speak to these wholesalers, be cooperative with them on their mailing lists. A bird dog is the same, but it just gives you directions. To turn the lead into a deal, you then get to follow-up. The bird dog will probably need a property license to pay them a finder's fee legally.

Cold Calls–This could be an effective method for those who can manage 50 rejections for each one successful phone call. For locating for sale by owner and for rent by owner listings, you can search the online classifieds or local paper. Then call the listings and ask questions one by one. Few people are going to do this, so you might find some gems that are passed by others.

Classified ads–You can advertise your service (buying property) online or in local print publications through free or low-cost classified ads. Not every avenue will work, but try as many as possible and get your information out there if they are low cost or free.

Real Estate Marketing Strategies to Expand Your Business

The real estate market is going through many ups and downs and is based on multiple factors, including interest rates, economic conditions, and job growth.

Regardless of the current nature of the industry, novices and pros can use other tactics that can push the company forward. This article looks at some of the main tactics that you can use to grow your real estate business.

Identify the target market

This is probably the number one strategy you can use as a real estate agent to become truly successful.

Several real estate brokers and companies focused on a niche market and becoming an industry specialist. This gives you an idea of what currently drives the target market, what risks it involves, and, most importantly where the short-and long-term market is headed.

For example, an immovable broker who knows the details of new local transportation or school project might change his marketing strategies accordingly.

Budget for marketing expenses

Another important factor in effectively expanding the real estate business is established and adhering to a marketing budget.

There are hundreds of ways to spend your dollars on marketing, such as real estate websites, email marketing, social media marketing, and postal marketing.

Your expenditure must be based on the target audience. For instance, customers in the bay area of San Francisco may need internet-based marketing, while customers in a rural area may need a different approach.

Create a website and use social media

Regardless of the business, with the help of a professional website, you need to build your presence on the internet as well as dedicated profiles on social media sites like Facebook, Twitter, and LinkedIn. These are relatively cheap, with the potential for extensive outreach.

You can also advertise your business by paying for ad campaigns on search engines such as Google and Bing.

Encourage referrals and word-of-mouth

By referrals from previous customers, the most successful real estate agents generate several deals. A recommendation from a client is most appreciated by a potential buyer or seller.

For example, when recommended by an acquaintance, boss, or family, new customers are more confident choosing a real estate agent. Through giving referral incentives to the individual recruiting a new customer, you can always improve this strategy.

Respond quickly

We live in a world that runs much faster than ever before. Responding to consumer requests is very critical. Otherwise, you risk losing new business.

You must always have access to email through a smartphone and ensure that you respond as soon as possible to a customer request. You can't wait in this company to respond until the next day. When you respond promptly, it adds credibility and prestige to your response.

Publish a real estate newsletter

If you're serious about your long-term success, then you might consider writing a weekly or monthly newsletter with information on current mortgage prices, improvements to real estate regulations, homeownership incentives, how to build a portfolio for real estate investment, local market health checks, etc.

Both current and prospective clients will enjoy such a newsletter's feedback as it demonstrates your business knowledge and dedication.

Dispel questions on the need for a real estate agent

Disintermediation refers to the way consumers talk about whether or not they need a real estate agent. Disintermediation advertising seeks to persuade those clients of the quality a real estate agent has to bring.

You may inform consumers about the need for a real estate agent and attorney during the selling or purchasing of a house or piece of land through your website or marketing channels.

Plan for success

Whether you're a real estate agent or a real estate developer, you're going to need a business plan for real estate development. This is going to set you up for success. With the help of a business plan for real estate development, you can plan your expenses, contingencies, and other risks.

Most people fail without such preparations while operating in a vacuum. For example, using a well-documented business plan, you will prepare the budget for next year's real estate marketing strategies.

Develop brand awareness

As big brand businesses, the real estate business always has to aspire to grow its name. This might be under the name of your name or the name of your company. Any method of real estate sales that you implement will bear in mind this definition.

People also ask how to sell immovable properties and how to build a business effectively. The response is to plan and build a brand name and use it for years to promote the company.

Conclusion

It takes effort and time to develop a successful real estate business. If followed carefully and diligently, the strategies listed in this chapter will be worth your effort.

Tips For Becoming A Successful Real Estate Agent

A lot of new real estate agents never do it in their first two years. Expenses were underestimated, and profits overestimated a deadly combination. Or they rely too heavily on old industry truisms that are not as valid in the real estate world that has developed since the financial meltdown of 2008-09 in the internet-driven decade. These three articles buck some of the traditional wisdom, unlocking fresh secrets for success in real estate.

You Don't Have to Be Good at "Sales."

There are ways of presenting yourself and managing your business that separate you from the image of a "pushy real estate salesperson." Excellent photography skills and the ability to write compelling listing descriptions will go far beyond selling skills. For better results, think of "consultant." Try to stay out of selling mode, even if you're desperate for a bargain.

Think Small for Big Success

Thinking low in this essay does not mean aiming for growth and success. It's about knowing your role as an independent contractor and being always in charge of your branding to make your company mobile, agile, and able to move and expand with you.

Develop a Business Plan and Stick to It

Your long-term success depends on many things, but one of the most important is a good start-up business plan.

Don't let your passion for seeing a customer right away deter you from planning and budgeting activities that are all-important. The tools and instructions here will help you focus on important business practices and build your prospect base quickly without spending a lot of money.

Develop a Budget, and Stick to That Too!

In your career as a real estate agent, it is important that you not only cover the costs of your real estate agent, but also the personal cost of living. Spread your personal living expenses and leave nothing out, including cash for fun or coffee out of the pocket.

You Don't Have to "List to Last"

You've read that: "If you're not selling, you're not going to last in real estate." It's a very old saying, and it originated in the very old world of real estate. Market and business have changed, and as a new real estate agent, or even through a whole career, you can be successful in working with buyers only and not listing properties as a seller's representative. Even if you do that, you will at least give more value to customers and a slightly better balance of your business income.

Maintain connections with past clients and referral sources

Kramer says buying lunch (typically $50 a meeting) four days a week for contacts offers around 10% return on investment, far more than the 2% return on investment he sees from blanketing postcard neighborhoods.

Sending former customers listing and updates from the open house can also pay dividends, Kramer said.

Never Assume

Passing the property test, receiving the license, and starting a new company is a big step. In their first year or two, most new real estate agents struggle, but you don't have to be one of them. It's about not making hypotheses and getting ready to hustle. For starters, don't assume you're going to start receiving lots of recommendation business from them because you've told all your family and friends about your new career. You shouldn't rely too much on the broker with which you hook up; just because you're now listed on the website or brochure doesn't mean leads are going to start pouring in.

On the other hand, in the brokerage department, you certainly get as much floor time as you can, even taking turns from others. Each walk-in is a contract that is opportunity. Don't look at any future. One new agent took on a walk-in that, because of his dirty and torn clothing, no one else in the office wanted to work with. He turned out to be the local trash hauling company's working owner—and the source of one of her first year's largest deals.

Hard Money Loans

To put it, Hard Money Lenders are non-institutional lenders issuing short-term loans to purchase an investment property, and sometimes to renovate it. Some also call them "hard-money borrowers." These private-money lenders are known for providing private-money loans to short-term fix-and-flippers as well as long-term investors pursuing venture capital, quick finance, or cash-out refinancing. Hard money mortgages can be obtained by real estate investors (or home flippers) who want to renovate and resell the properties used as lending collateral–often within a year, if not earlier. The higher cost of a hard money loan is offset by the fact that the borrower intends to pay off the loan relatively quickly–most hard money loans are for one to three years–and by some of the other advantages they offer If you need a private money lender to finance your next investment in real estate, there are numerous private money lending homes offering competitive prime rates. The downside of using private money lenders is that they do not accept any fees for advance payment. And in a very short time you can get sponsored, which saves you a lot of time. In reality, within fifteen days, you can get fully funded. It takes just a few minutes to prequalify online. There are several reasons why investors in real estate choose to use lenders of hard money. The main reason is the lender's ability to finance the loan quickly. Hard money loans can be financed in most situations in a matter of days or with a week as opposed to the 30–45 days it takes for a bank loan to be financed. Sometimes it usually takes a day or two to apply for a hard money mortgage, and in some situations a loan can be accepted the same day. The ability to obtain financing at a much faster rate than a bank loan is a significant advantage for a borrower in real estate. Especially when the real estate investor tries to purchase a property with many competing bids, a quick closure with a hard money loan will attract the attention of a seller and set their offer apart from the other buyers offering slow conventional financing.

Such hard-money lenders, or personal hard-money lenders, provide a high-rate, short-term loan that will pay all costs based on your contract agreement, including acquisition and maintenance costs. Generally, however, they are also more hierarchical and semi-institutional. We were also frequently allowed to lend to investors.

The word "hard work" is a misnomer, and it doesn't mean you'd have trouble getting sponsored. It's pretty easy. The word arises as the mortgage is dependent on the asset involved. You want to make sure the house is deemed appealing before you lend, and the more attractive the home is, the more likely it is that you will get a mortgage.

Hard money loans are secured by a 30% to 50% equity property, so the investor is also protected.

A hard money loan is a bridge loan for the short term. This method of loan is very successful and, due to the advantages mentioned above, dominated most real estate transactions. Unlike the traditional loan process where your creditworthiness matters, private hard money borrowers rely solely on your asset's price. Since conventional borrowers, such as banks, have no experience in hard-money lending, hard-money lenders are often private individuals or organizations that see potential in this form of risky venture.

Private money loans or "private hard money loans" are a great investment option for you regardless of your experience level. It is perfect for real estate investors, both existing and experienced. The system provides a much better and more efficient forum for accredited investors to clarify complex but transactions.

The cost to the borrower of a hard money loan is typically higher than the funding available by banks or government credit schemes, reflecting the higher risk the lender is taking in providing the funding. The added cost, though, is a tradeoff for quicker capital entry, a less restrictive approval process, and greater consistency in the repayment schedule.

For restructuring scenarios and in funding short-term investments for lenders with low creditworthiness but considerable equity in their assets, hard money loans are usually very useful.

Private hard money borrowers provide an ideal opportunity to find flexible and competitive real estate mortgages for real estate investors. Generally, they have a wide range of general business expertise and, also, knowledge of banking and real estate. Since hard money loans can be issued easily, it is easy to use a hard money loan as a means to stave off foreclosure.

10 Must-Knows Facts about Hard Money Loans

Hard money loans from private investors are one of the best sources of funding for investors who want to take advantage of the great real-market prices. They make it possible for you to buy real options, even in today's limited lending market with competitive terms and conditions on one to four-unit homes.

Here are ten things you should know about these fun items for financing:

- Hard money loans help secure and make it possible to tough transactions. We are your best option if you have a slam-dunk deal that is not going to pass scrutiny with a bank.
- They're better than you thought. While hard money typically costs more than a bank loan, most borrowers can get loans at rates and terms that are very favorable. The mortgage is quite cheap, considering the returns that most real estate investors expect to make on assets bought with hard money.
- Cash reserves are significant. Many private borrowers, no matter what, want to make sure you have enough money to support their mortgage.
- Private loans can also be used for non-Immobiliare purchases. Private loans can also be used to finance

construction and rehabilitation projects as well as direct purchases.

- There are fast hard money loans. Instead of months, you can expect to close your loan in days or weeks. While loans typically take two to three weeks to close, it is possible to close in three days.
- Lenders of hard money are elastic. Because they are private individuals, loans can often be uniquely tailored to suit specific needs.
- Flips, rehabs, and other sales of troubled assets are not a concern. They are a perfect opportunity for a private lender because they make you money as a borrower.
- Access to private mortgage loans makes getting the best rates better for you. Being able to buy without a contingency of loans or with a very short contingency of loans makes you a much more attractive buyer with a lot of upsides to the sellers of distressed property.
- Hard money loans are available on an interest-based basis only with 30-year amortization terms or, in the case of short-term loans. This will encourage you to use more cash flow to make more investments.
- Private mortgage holders seem to be more concerned about your reputation than about your credit score. Although you must be creditworthy, most private lenders will not immediately dismiss you on the grounds of your FICO score alone.

There are options to choose a hard money lender in search of an immovable loan:

Business Experience

Investing in real estate is not easy if you start. It requires a wide variety of techniques and action courses and best practices that you may not be familiar with, especially if you are a newbie. Hard money lenders should help you study and evaluate a deal's specifics and appreciate the workings in a comprehensive way for you to make an informed decision. This uses a business model that is quite different from traditional lenders ' business model. Alternatively, a creditor of private money can only base his judgment on the merits of the contract. You don't have to worry about security with hard money lenders. It should be stressed, in particular, that you get money from legal and reliable sources. Contracts are contractual, and the creditor may focus on fulfilling the deal's specifications. In a real estate deal, all conventional protections are followed so that both the lender and the creditor may make informed decisions and act accordingly.

Capital Availability

One of the main issues traditional money lenders face when financing a deal is the availability of capital and its low-risk tolerance. On the other hand, private hard money lenders are not restricted by a loan committee's risk tolerance or government regulation. If the lender believes the interest rate justifies the risk, he will be able to make any deal he wants. In highly lucrative but unconventional real estate deals, this fact is particularly important. Thousands of private money lenders are looking for these kinds of deals.

There is typically a broad link between extremely reliable and respected third-party lenders who tie together investors and private hard money loans. The deals, investors, and borrowers are vetted by these firms. Moreover, by providing access to a wide range of borrowers, brokers, realtors, and investors, they can add value to your business part.

Usually, hard money lenders analyze each lending system using a case-by-case model and assess the asset's worth. Therefore, as opposed to the traditional underwriting process characteristic of traditional money lenders, there is the likelihood of compromise. It is also possible to negotiate payment schedules for a loan, and usually the opportunity is given to borrowers to look for opportunities to repay the loan during the extension period. A very big advantage of obtaining funding by hard money borrowers is the presence of a large number of accredited investors willing to invest in backed real-estate transactions than ordinary banks won't or won't be able to back up. For a complicated but otherwise sound deal, not having access to traditional bank funds should not be an end. In other words, in the aggressive quest for outstanding, real-estate secured opportunities, there is a large amount of capital.

In contrast, borrowers of hard money are also very receptive. That is, they have accredited investors who have been involved at the executive level in their own business or a company. They understand how to make sound business decisions that are going to suit both parties. There is no problem with traditional financing operations such as bureaucracy, extensive documentation and time-consuming. In other words, borrowers can trust that in the shortest possible time they will have a response without the need for the investor to confer with committees or supervisory boards.

Flexible Financing

Bank loans and other traditional real estate loans are usually subject to rigid terms and conditions that could scare the average beginner away from real estate engagement. On the other hand, hard money loans have fewer restrictions and are less restrictive as well. Only to protect your wellbeing are their rules, legislation, and procedures. However, the financial terms of the deal are entirely up to the parties concerned. Also, the process of approving a hard money loan is often much faster than applying for a mortgage or applying for financing through a bank through conventional traditional loans. Because of their business experience, private investors who back the hard money loan can make informed decisions faster and often do not carry out credit checks or examine the credit history of a borrower. Therefore, the actions that borrowers usually take to examine the willingness of a borrower to meet loan payments are robust and even start-up-friendly. Such creditors are not as worried about getting compensation because if the borrower defaults, they may have a much higher value and ability to resell the assets themselves. In most cases, lenders would only have to request a reasonable plan or a structured curriculum that explains in detail how they expect to pay off the loan.

In contrast, private money loans generally require less documentation and less confirmation resulting in a system that is much easier and cheaper than traditional lending. This can be particularly important in situations where time is essential, such as investors who are trying to close a major purchase or property owners who are due shortly to have a looming balloon payment or another large cash deadline. Since private money loans are focused almost entirely on the value of collateral from the mortgage, private money lenders are more prone to lending to poor credit, creditors, or to unusual assets from which traditional lenders are wary. Private money borrowers can also choose from various loan term options and may be open to negotiating their fees and interest rates in some situations.

Interest Rates and Points for Hard Money Loans are Flexible and Affordable

The interest rates and points paid by borrowers for hard money will range from lender to lender and vary from region to region as well. For example, property flippers living in the U.S. are well aware that hard money borrowers in California typically have lower rates than other parts of the country since there are many hard money lending companies in California. Increased competition leads to lower costs. Interest rates are equivalent to many traditional bank loans when calculating both charges and costs. Yet hard money borrowers have terms and conditions that are not set in stone, and the requirements can be adjusted to suit the lender's priorities and needs.

Hard money lenders are prepared to take on more risk than conventional bank loans with their loans. It should be expected that their increased willingness to take on higher risk will result in higher interest rates than conventional loans for a hard money loan. Interest rates for hard money loans usually range from 10-15% depending on the particular lender, the perceived risk of the loan, and the value of the asset. Points will vary from 2% to 4% of the total loan volume everywhere. Based on the loan to value ratio, interest rates and points can vary greatly. Numerous studies have confirmed that the difficulties in securing funding through traditional financing institutions are often due to the limited institutional or government requirements that many traditional banks decline to fund an otherwise excellent real estate deal. Individual investors are not required to follow the same procedures and can make informed decisions based solely on the merits of the offer.

The amount of loan that the hard money lender will lend is usually calculated by the debt sum ratio divided by a property's value. This is referred to as the interest lending (LTV). Most hard money borrowers are going to lend up to 65–75 percent of the property's current value, which is a lot of courses. Some lenders will lend based on the value after repair (ARV) which is the property's estimated value after the borrower has improved the property. It generates a more expensive mortgage from the standpoint of the hard money creditor as the amount of capital the lender brings in rises, and the amount of capital spent by the borrower reduces. The increased risk would result in a higher interest rate being paid by the hard money lender.

There are some hard money borrowers who are going to lend a high percentage of the ARV and even cover the expenses of recovery. This may sound great to begin with from the borrower's point of view, but there is a much higher risk involved in these types of loans and the interest rate and points will be much higher. If a creditor finances a mortgage with little or no down payment from the borrower, you should expect an interest rate of around 15%–18% and 5 –6 points.

How to Get a Hard Money Lender to Work With

There are many ways to find a reliable provider with hard money. One easy way to find a local lender of hard money is to search for[your area] + "hard money lenders." In the search results, there will be individual companies as well as lists of hard money lenders compiled by others. This will provide a good number of lenders to start contacting them for evaluation and shortlisting. You can then start contacting them after this is over. To evaluate their credibility, you must read their reviews.

Another way to find a hard money lender is to attend the club meeting of your local real estate investor. These club meetings are held in most cities and are usually well attended by lenders of hard money looking to network with potential borrowers. If there are no hard money borrowers at the conference, ask other real estate investors if they can suggest a hard money lender. Real estate brokers, conventional mortgage brokers, and other practitioners in the real estate sector may be able to refer an experienced lender of hard money. Take advantage of your existing network and see who is best recommended.

Once you have compiled a list of a few borrowers, it is time to start calling them and choosing the most appropriate lender to finance your next contract.

Typically, hard money borrowers grant short-term real estate loans that were used to purchase and renovate an investment property. For both short-term fix-and-flip investors and long-term buy-and-hold investors, hard money loans are good.

Hard money borrowers are known to be private creditors "third-party," which in terms of relationship is the most distant from a creditor. Hard money borrowers, however, are regarded as the best private lenders because they are the most reputable and have fixed interest rates, prices, charges, and conditions on loans.

In this section, we refer to hard money lenders as private money lenders. The reason that private lenders are referred to as lenders of hard money is not far-fetched. This is because hard money loans usually have short loan terms ranging from 1 to 3 years, interest rates ranging from 7% to 12%, and lending charges varying from 1.5% to 10%.

In the primary or second-degree circles of a borrower, on the other hand, private lenders have loan terms, rates, and costs that vary widely.

Features Of A Profitable Investment Property

Are you looking for a residential investment rental property to purchase? For a first-time investor, the idea can be daunting. Real estate is a tough business, and it's peppered with land mines that can wipe out your returns. While shopping for an income property, here are the most important things to consider.

You may want a real estate agent to help you complete the purchase, but you should start your search for a property. A broker could put unnecessary pressure on you to buy before you consider an investment that best suits you. And it will take some sleuthing expertise and some shoe leather to locate the money.

Your scope will be constrained by whether you intend to manage the property directly or to employ someone else to handle it. You don't want a house that's too far from where you live if you're going to manage it actively. If you want to take care of a property management company, proximity is less of a problem.

Let's look at the top 10 things you can take into account when searching for the right rental property.

Top 10 A Profitable Rental Property Highlights

The Location

The neighborhood you are buying will determine the types of tenants you are attracting and the vacancy rate. When you buy near a university, the odds are that your pool of potential renters will be filled by students, and you will struggle to fill vacancies each summer. You should also be mindful that some towns are trying to discourage lease sales by enforcing exorbitant license fees and piling on the bureaucracy.

Taxes on land

Property taxes are likely to vary significantly in the target area, and you want to know how much you are going to lose from them. In a great neighborhood, which attracts long-term tenants, high property taxes are not always a bad thing, but there are also lousy places with high taxes. The appraisal department of the city will have all the tax information on record or you can speak to local homeowners. It is also wise to find out whether increases in property tax are likely to occur shortly. A city in financial distress can raise taxes far beyond what a landlord can rent realistically.

Schools

Consider the quality of local schools if you're dealing with family-sized homes. While you're mostly concerned about the monthly cash flow, when you eventually sell it, the overall value of your rental property comes into play. It can affect the value of your investment if there are no good schools nearby.

Crime Rate

No one wants to live next door for criminal activity at a hot spot. Local police or public library should have precise neighborhood crime statistics. Check vandalism, serious crimes, and small-scale crime rates, and see if criminal activity moves up or down. You may also want to ask about the frequency of your neighborhood's police presence.

Demand for the work

Locations with growing opportunities for employment draw more residents. Consult with the U.S. to figure out how a work quality region ranks. Work statistics office or go to a local library. If you see an announcement that a big company is moving to the area, you can be sure that employees are flocking to the area in search of a place to live. This can result in house prices rising or falling, depending on the type of company that comes in. You can presume that if you want the business in your house, it will also be your landlord.

Apps

Tour the community to scope out the parks, cafes, gyms, movie theaters, public transport connections, and all the other advantages that landlords are receiving. City Hall may have promotional literature to give you an idea of where you can find the best mix of public amenities and private property.

Design for the future

The Department of Municipal Planning will have information on the coming or zoning of new development in the area. It's probably a good growth area if there's a lot of construction going on. Watch out for new developments that might damage nearby properties ' values. You could also compete with your estate with additional new homes.

Amount of openings or listings

If there are an unusually high number of listings in a community, it can either signify a decreasing seasonal period or area. You have to figure out what it is. High vacancy rates in either case force landlords to lower rents to attract tenants.

Average incomes

Rental income is going to be your go to, so you need to learn what the area's average rent is. Make sure that any estate you feel would bear enough rent to cover your mortgage payment, taxes, and other expenses. Study the region well enough to assess where in the next five years it will be gone. If you can afford the region now, but it is anticipated that taxes will increase, an inexpensive estate today will later mean bankruptcy.

Human cataclysms

Insurance is another burden you need to deduct from your dividends, so you need to know how much it will cost you. If an area is prone to earthquakes or floods, the rental income can eat away the cost of insurance.

Getting the Information

Official sources are great, but to get the real scoop, talk to the neighbors. Talk to both landlords and homeowners. In the negative aspects, investors will be much more straightforward because they have no interest in it. Visit the area to see your future neighbors in action at different times on different days of the week.

Choosing a property

In general, a single-family residence or condominium is the best investment property for beginners. Condos are low maintenance as they take care of exterior renovations by the condo association, leaving you to think about the interior instead. However, condos tend to accumulate lower rents and appreciate more slowly than single-family homes.

Long-term tenants tend to be attracted to single-family homes. Families or couples are generally better tenants than individuals because they are more likely to be financially stable and regularly pay the rent.

Look for a house that has the potential for growth and better-estimated cash flow when you have the area narrowed down. Search for more expensive properties than you can afford as well as those within your control. Immovable assets often sell under their listing price.

To appreciate the potential, you are looking for a property that will attract tenants who are willing to pay higher rents, with a few cosmetic changes and some renovations. This will also increase the property's value if, after a few years, you choose to sell it.

Of course, purchasing a reasonably priced property is a key step in ensuring a profitable effort. The rental property guideline is to pay no more than twelve times the annual rent that you expect to receive.

Setting the rent So how do you determine potential rent? You'll have to make an informed guess. With overly optimistic assumptions, don't get carried away. Setting the rent too high and ending up chipping away at the overall profit in a hurry with an empty unit for months.

Start with the neighborhood's average rent and work from there. Consider if it's worth a little more or a little less, and why.

To determine if the rent number works for you as an investor, find out what the place will cost you. Subtract your expected monthly mortgage payment, 12-month divided property taxes, 12-divided insurance costs, and a generous maintenance and repair allowance.

Do not neglect the maintenance and repair costs. These costs depend on the property's age and how much you're planning to do. It is possible that a new building would take less than an existing one. It is doubtful that an apartment in a seniors' building would experience the same amount of damage as off-campus college housing.

Cutting costs considerably in making your repairs, but it also means being on call 24/7 for emergencies. Another possibility is to hire a property management company. Each month, the company handles everything from faulty toilets to rent collection. Expect to pay about 10 percent of this service's gross rental income.

If all these figures come out, or better yet, with a little leftover, you can now get an offer from your real estate agent.

Making the Purchase

Banks have tougher demands for investment property loans than for primary residences. They assume that when times get tough, people are less likely than a business property to jeopardize their homes. Be prepared to pay for a down payment plus closing costs at least 20 percent to 30 percent. Have a contractor check the properties carefully and have an attorney review all before signing.

Don't forget insurance for homeowners. Renter's insurance covers the property of a tenant, but the property itself is the responsibility of the landlord, and the insurance may be more expensive than a similar owner-occupied home. The mortgage, insurance, and depreciation of the property are all tax-deductible up to a certain amount.

Every state has good cities, every city has good neighborhoods, and there are good properties in every neighborhood. To align all three, it takes a lot of footwork and research.

Once you find your dream rental property, keep your expectations reasonable, and make sure your finances are reasonably stable to wait for the estate to start generating money instead of desperately needing it.

Keys To Successfully Invest In A Real Estate

To assess a rental property, when you follow these five criteria, you should be well-positioned to handle a lot of common real estate investment pitfalls.

Sure, so you decided to invest in a rental property. Investing in real estate generally offers investors several benefits ranging from a steady income, someone else's support paying down the mortgage debt, the opportunity to use equity, and lucrative growth opportunities.

When you buy in the long term, real estate can be a good investment. Home flippers and renovators can also make a profit, of course, but the rental business follows other principles than a short-sighted gamble that depends on a fast dollar.

If you want to invest in a rental property, particularly if you're a real estate investor for the first time, there are a few simple investing guidelines that should stop you from diving into a few potentially expensive minefields.

Most enter the real estate investment world, but not everyone becomes a successful investor in real estate. Why is that? Well, while the best way to build wealth is to make money in real estate, investing in real estate is not as simple as buying a rental property and waiting for it to start generating profits. Successful investors invest their money, as well as their time and energy when it comes to investing in real estate. In particular, there are some primary performance indicators that need to be addressed before purchasing an investment property and beginning an investing career. Now, let's delve into the key factors that should be known to every real estate investor for a successful real estate investment career without further ado.

Real Estate Investing Success Factor:

Position, Any real estate investor, seems to have learned the position is the key factor in real estate investment success. Indeed, successful property investors would often say that before buying an investment property, the three most important factors to consider are: location, location, location! But why is that?

First, there's a constant location. You may change a lot of things about an investment property as a real estate investor, but the one thing you can't change is the location of your income property! In the geographic area where you buy an investment property before you sell it, you're stuck.

The second reason that position in real estate investment is critical is that it dictates the supply and demand: successful real estate developers are always searching for areas with fair supply and high demand. The location's supply and demand further decide how much rental income you will pay for your income property and how much it will cost you to work. As a consequence, the viability of your rental property will be decided.

Finally, in real estate investment, the position is a crucial success driver because it decides value! The land is a limited resource, constituting a large portion of an investment property's price, and in the future some locations will appreciate more.

Generally speaking, what makes a good place for investment in real estate is a low supply and high demand for investment properties, relatively low running costs of buying an investment property, high rental income, and anticipated market appreciation.

How can you find a good location for investment in real estate with the features listed above? No worries, the rental property calculator from Mashvisor is going to be of great help in this regard! Click here to start searching and analyzing the best investment properties to choose from in your city and neighborhood.

Real Estate Investing Success Factor:

Positive cash flow In the investment of real estate, positive cash flow is the profit from a rental property made every month. The main reason why positive cash flow is a key factor in success is simply that the higher the difference between rental income and rental expenses, the better the return on investment rate. Successful property investors are always looking for positive cash flowing investment properties because the real estate investor would still make money through rental income until the economy recovers, even when the real estate market is declining. Positive cash flows also tend to increase over time, enabling income property investors to make even more money from investing in real estate with each year that passes.

Also, positive cash flow disburses the mortgage of a real estate investor, leading to an increase in the equity of the income property! Not only that, but successful property investors can save additional income from positive cash flow to be used as down payment to purchase another investment property. Positive cash flow is, therefore, a crucial success driver for investing in real estate because it helps buyers to purchase and own several investment properties!

Real Estate Investing Success Factor:

Financial Assessment. Another significant success factor for real estate investment is a financial assessment and awareness of the financial aspects of rental property ownership. There are various ways for funding the purchase of an investment estate– mortgage loans, private money lenders, hard money lenders, etc. Before deciding how to finance their investment properties, successful property investors always analyze the requirements and outputs of each method.

Other things that should be familiar to a real estate investor include rental property taxes, payment plans and calculation of mortgages. Always identify your current financial situation, your personal financial goals, and the maximum amount of loan to which you are eligible for successful real estate investment, and set a budget before purchasing an investment property so that you are not financially distracted.

Real Estate Investing Performance Factor:

Rental Strategy One of the decisions a real estate investor has to make in the real estate investment environment is which rental strategy–conventional and Airbnb–to adopt. Many income property owners choose the conventional rental approach because they feel that rentals from Airbnb are too expensive and too much effort. However, the location of your rental property is what determines which rental strategy is the best. Some areas are suitable for traditional rent, while others are more suitable for Airbnb.

The reason why a success factor in real estate investment is determining the rental strategy is that the rental strategy will ultimately affect your investment return rate. For example, a successful real estate investor will invest in an Airbnb (short-term) rental while investing in a rental property in an area with a strong tourism industry because it would produce higher returns than a typical (long-term) rental.

Property management

Great property management is another key success factor in real estate investment. It takes time, organization, social skills, and attention to detail to manage income property. We don't mean finding tenants by property management and collecting monthly rent. In addition to conducting a tenant screening process to find the best tenants, you need to determine the best way to advertise your investment property—the ideal tenant is one who pays monthly rent and does not damage the rental property.

Also, property management requires an investor in real estate to keep track of repairs, maintain the rental property, and deal with any problems that tenants may have. As an investor in real estate, if you don't have the time and energy you need to manage property, then investment in real estate is probably not your best career option.

Hiring professional property management is an alternative to property management and successful real estate investment! There are many specialist property management firms (such as Pillow) that are specialized in handling investment properties and supplying property investors with a set of services including sales, leasing, rental, renovations, and upkeep. Nevertheless, keep in mind that they come at a price.

Investing in Real Estate is one of the best ways to make money, but that doesn't mean it's an easy career. The time and energy they put into their investments are what distinguishes successful property investors from the average ones. Also, each real estate investor must know and take into consideration the above-mentioned main success factors if he/she wants to join the category of successful real estate income investors.

How To Correctly Value And Analyze Investment Property

There is no easy way, unlike stocks, to determine the exact value of your current property or the property you plan to buy. As a multi-property owner, I'm happy that there are no ticker symbols that jump around every weekday because they're just a distraction.

It's all about buying, maintaining, and holding as long as possible to build wealth when it comes to real estate.

Currently, real estate accounts for about 35-40 percent of my net worth, where it will stay for the foreseeable future as I focus on business efforts. Instead of chasing unicorns on the stock market, earnings that came from focusing on my career were largely reinvested in real estate for diversification purposes.

I'm going to approach valuing property from the standpoint of an investor in this chapter. We're going to go through some big-picture concepts and use an example of real-life to see if we're making a good or bad investment. I think you're going to enjoy this estate I've picked. If you are already a homeowner, with as realistic an eye as possible, you will approach valuing your property.

Valuing Property – Big Picture Fundamentals

It's all about earnings

As an investor in real estate, you need to find out what realistic income the target property can generate year in and year out on a sustainable basis. The most important thing is the current and historical figures of income.

Once you have an income range, you can calculate the gross rental yield and income valuation price of a property to compare with other neighborhood properties.

The appreciation of the price is secondary

One of the big reasons for a housing bubble and then a recession was because buyers were moving away from the property's income element and focused on future property appreciation. Investors didn't care if they could ride the wave and flip for profits within a year or two, they would be hugely cashflow negative.

Speculators were crushed once the party stopped, causing a domino effect, hurting those neighbors who were planning to buy and hold. If you focus primarily on the appreciation of the property and not on income, you are a speculator. If it does not generate income or save an individual on rent, there is no real value of real estate.

Generally, property prices rise sharply with inflation

The appreciation of property prices generally tracks inflation by +/-2%. In other words, if the current inflation rate is 3 percent, you can predict the national property prices to rise by 1-5 percent. Naturally, changes in property prices can fluctuate wildly over the years. But you will see a relatively smooth correlation when you look at property prices over ten years.

Once you tend to predict steady annual price gains of 10 percent, you are delusional. Remember that the appreciation of property prices should be considered as a secondary attribute. If it happens, perfect. If not, the focus will be on your cash flow.

Ownership is always local

Be careful not to extrapolate data on the land. Just because one report says property prices in San Francisco are rising 19.6 percent year-over-year in May does not mean that I will be selling my home for 19.6 percent more. My home price maybe 10 percent higher because it's higher than the median. You can also throw out the national window statistics.

If your neighbor sells the best price to find out what your home is worth. Statistics of property prices show you the general price trend and the relative strength zones.

Specific Steps To Value Your Property Correctly

Calculate your gross annual rental income

Take the reasonable monthly rent from comparable that you find online and divide by 12 to get your annual rent. Now take the annual gross rent and divide by the property's market price. For example, $2,000 per month= $24,000 per year. $24,000/$500,000= 4.8% gross rent. The annual gross rental yield is to get a quick apple snapshot of what the blue sky potential is for a property if you pay 100% cash and don't have ongoing expenses.

Compare the net rent with the risk-free price

The 10-year bond yield is the risk-free price. Investors say "risk-free" because there is almost 0 chance that their debt obligations will be defaulted by the US government. All investments require a risk premium over the risk-free rate; otherwise, why bother to risk investing your money. If the property's annual gross rental yield is lower than the risk-free rate, either negotiate harder or move on.

Calculate your net rent (cap rate) per year

The gross rental income is simply the net operating income split by the property's market value. Through calculating your annual gross lease minus mortgage interest, premiums, property taxes, HOA dues, marketing, and maintenance costs, I like to measure net operating income. In other words, we measure the real annual profit bottom line.

Compare the net rental yield to the risk free rate

Ideally, the net rent rate should be equivalent to or higher than the free rate of risk. With time, you will pay the principal down, thus increasing the net rental yield and spreading the risk-free rate. If everything goes well, rentals will also go up, and you will enjoy your house.

In Nevada, Florida, California, and Arizona, there are plenty of properties with net rental yields several percentage points higher than the current risk-free rate after the collapse. The reason they were not being snatched up by more consumers in 2010-2012 was that investors often had to pay cash because banks were not borrowing.

Calculate the property's price-to-earnings ratio

The P / E ratio is your property's market value divided by the actual net operating profit. In the above $500,000/$4,700 example= 106. Woah! It will take a net operating profit owner 106 years to make his or her investment back! This assumes that the owner never pays off his mortgage and does not see a highly unlikely increase in rents.

For a blue sky example, a better way to calculate it is to get the net rental income split by the property's market value= $500,000/$24,000= 20.8. The better for the buyer, the lower the P / E, and the better for the seller vice versa.

Property price projection and plans for rent

Only moments are the P / E ratio and rental yields. The real opportunity is to anticipate expectations properly. You want to take advantage of fear and unfortunate situations like a divorce, a relocation of a company, a layoff, a bankrupt city, or a natural disaster as a real estate investor. You want to sell the illusion of ever-increasing prices as a real estate retailer.

The best way to predict the future is to compare what happened in the past by digital maps offered by DataQuick, Redfin, and Zillow and have realistic expectations of local job creation. Should workers move or leave the city? Is the city allowing tons of land to grow or have restrictions like building heights? Is the city in financial trouble and asking for more property taxes for owners?

Run various scenarios

The final step is to get an accurate lease and property cost estimates and run different scenarios. If rents fall at a rate of 5 percent a year for five years, are you going to be OK? When mortgage rates increase from 3.5 percent to 5 percent over five years for 30-year fixed mortgages, what will this do to demand? If the main value falls by another 20%, will I jump off a bridge?

Ideally, not if you reside in one of the non-recourse countries where the keys can be recovered and your other property secured. Always run at your bare minimum, a bearish case, realistic case, and bullish case scenario.

Pay heed to taxation and depreciation

Nearly all expenses related to owning a rental property, including mortgage interest and property tax, are tax-deductible. The confusion lies in the phase-out of the income-based deductions (another article: Limit Depends on Income Mortgage Deduction). What is also interesting to understand is depreciation, a non-cash item that reduces your net operating income (depreciation is a non-cash cost), to reduce your income, but also your tax bill.

Be conscious, however, still focus on the actual bottom line currency. $250,000 in individuals' earnings and $500,000 in married couples' income are tax-free if you live in the property for two of the last five years. There is also the 1031 exchange that allows investors to transfer proceeds to another property without making any gains and, thus, taxes. While the tax code is complex, it supports property owners at the margin.

Test comparable sales at all times

Punching in the property address of Zillow.com is the best way to check comparable sales over the last six to twelve months. On the lower right side, you'll see the tax records, the revenue history, and comparable.

You need to equate the asking price of your desired estate to previous sales and assess it against what has improved since you get a good deal.

Valuing Property Is Part Science Part Guess Work
More open houses and transactions that you follow from beginning to end, the more comfortable you will get with the exercise of property values assessment. It almost becomes a sixth sense in which you know instinctively whether or not the estate is a good deal. For a couple of months, anyone looking to buy property should hit the weekly open houses to get a feel for your local market.

How Find Rental Properties

How to find a property for rent? That's a question that any real estate investor would at some point in the Google search bar hoping to quickly find a result that would serve his / her search purposes and help him/her find house rentals or whatever type of rental property the investor is most interested in.

Nonetheless, this may be more difficult than it seems. For example, typing "rental properties near me" will give you thousands of results to choose from, with several rental websites and similar services offered by businesses, and with each at a different level of reliability and information consistency, finding the perfect app or platform is an even bigger challenge than finding the perfect rental property.

So how can you find the best way to seek properties that suit your quest expectations and parameters perfectly?

There are many different ways in which buyers will be able to find residential properties for sale. By using a variety of resources to locate assets, you give yourself the greatest opportunity to find the best investment option for you. Find Rental Property by Networking, and this is a great way to find rental properties that may not be known to the general public. You may be able to buy these assets at a lower price because they are not open to everyone. Useful networking teams with the following:

Personal Investor Network

This is the investor database that you either have accumulated over the months or years you've been investing in, or it's the database that you should start keeping forward from this point. It can include other property owners you've met who own rental property on the same street as you or an old college friend who's also a shareholder.

Investment Clubs

Investment clubs are useful contact because members often share and advertise properties for sale on an email list. If you don't belong to anybody, joining one may be a good idea. For an annual membership fee between $100 and $300, you can typically join a real estate investment club.

Personal Acquaintances/Relationships

Immobilities are not the only ones who can lead you to a big investment. Family, families, and professional contacts, such as attorneys and accountants, can be a great resource for future investments. They may be facing financial hardship, such as a short sale or bankruptcy, know someone who is, or has seen and read about a property for sale. We may also have their friends who want to unload real estate or who hear about a good opportunity to invest in real estate. Also, your contractors are a potential source for finding leads as they can work for other investors looking to sell off-market real estate.

Find Rental Property Online

You can search for a potential investment property on many different websites. These sites offer a variety of resources from general searches for sale to more specific searches for' short sale' and' foreclosure.' There are also sites offering property records and information about the area that can help you assess the investment property. There are even sites where live housing auctions can be bidden.

Find Rental Property Through Realtors

There are several ways you can use Realtors in your search for rental properties.

- For listings you are driving or viewing online, you can call the listing agent.
- To ask about potential investment property prospects, you can talk to real estate companies, and in particular Realtors named in certain towns and areas of towns.
- In some locations, listing agents will not always announce MLS listings. Some agents will only provide their actual contacts with these listings, so you need to be in the Realtor database as a contact to make those semi-off-market properties known.
- Realtors have access to the MLS and may or may not be listed on Realtor.dot with their MLS database.

Find Rental Property in Print Media

A great way to search for local listings is to print newspapers. You may not be advertising some of these properties online so that you won't have as much competition for them.

- Newspapers-Newspapers are a great source to find properties that are listed as Realtor properties for sale by owners. Look at your chosen region's main newspaper, as

well as smaller community newspapers that are more tailored to specific cities.
- Regional Advertising Journals-In many grocery stores; you can find these smaller journals. These are also a great source for locating homes since Realtor offices also advertise in these pamphlets their listings.

Find Rental Property at Auctions

Auctions on a property can be a great place to find a property deal. There are various types of auctions.

Online Auctions

Online auction sites such as Auction.dot, you can check for investment properties.

Sheriff Sale Auctions

Such sales are usually performed in the city hall of your county, registry hall, jail, or even in the office of the Sheriff. At these sales, foreclosures were sold to the general public for the first time. If the foreclosure doesn't purchased at the auction, then the foreclosing lender will take possession of the property and usually list the property with a local Realtor as an REO (real estate owned).

Private Auction Companies

Usually, creditors fund these auctions to sell large numbers of property at one time. Generally, these auctions are well advertised and carried out at a local hotel or conference center.

Summary

With a very wide selection of rental websites and media to choose from, it became part of the project of each real estate investor to begin by finding the best websites to locate rental properties before he/she even started planning the purchase.

Every prospective real estate investor to look out and determine whether he/she decides to use it to locate rental properties, as the platform can provide investors with all the resources they need to identify and choose the best rental property for their purchase. The value of rental listings is assured based on accurate data mining and historical comps, making it one of the best rental properties online options.

How To Finance Rental Properties

Are you comfortable with the rental property funding process? Do you feel like you grasp the various elements that you need to manage the financing of rental property?

It's no surprise we're seeing buyers come out in record numbers with the spring real estate market running on all cylinders. Real estate exit strategies have become incredibly attractive in today's housing industry, spanning from retail sales to complete rehabs. Specifically, one strategy seems to be in a great place; however: buy and hold rental property. Opportunities for cash flow are through the roof, as rents rise in almost every city from San Diego to New York. However, there will only be opportunities for those familiar with the ins and outs of rental property financing.

Don't Finance A Rental Property Before Considering These 4 Important Factors Now maybe one of the best times ever to purchase a rental property because of the heavy tax deductions and the positive impact it can have on your investment portfolio. Those who still have to do this, however, should be mindful of due diligence and consider what they get into before they make the jump. You need to find the right tenants, decide if you want a property manager or not, and make the necessary updates while maintaining the basic maintenance of the rental property. While there is a myriad of things that potential landlords should consider before they fund their first rental property, I strongly recommend starting with the following four:

- Numbers: Run your numbers before you try to finance a rental property, including transaction fees, management fees, and market indicators.

- Location: indicators such as neighborhood desirability and local amenities are important factors to look for when choosing a rental property.
- Tenants: finding and placing great tenants can make or break a rental property's financial health.
- Your Credit: Different borrowers will have different eligibility requirements, and it is necessary to check your credit score and background when trying to fund an estate.

Financing Rental Property: The Numbers

Prospective buyers will have to run the numbers to see how much they can afford to spend before they even consider looking at houses. Four very important factors must be well understood: finance, demand forecasts, transaction fees, and management fees. Let's take a closer look at each of these items individually:

Financing: if you can't close with money, you'll want to get acquainted with the funding options that are likely to be available to you at the moment. For that matter, nothing will have a greater impact on how your future deal is going to happen, or even what deal you are doing. Pay attention to your due diligence and examine your choices. Speak to a mortgage broker at the very least to figure out how much money you might have at your hands. You will also want to figure out how much of a deposit you will need to pay to receive reasonable monthly premiums at this stage of the process. Don't be afraid to browse around either; if you're willing to look for it, there's a loan with your name on it. This also applies if your rental property is to be refinanced. Additionally, alternative methods of finance are available, including the use of a hard or private money lender.

Transaction fees: Never assume there is no business cost; no one works free of charge. Don't forget to take into account taxes, legal fees, stamp duties, and any other additional costs that may accompany anything you intend to do. I strongly recommend that you carry out your research; each state is synonymous with its own set of individual fees. I urge you, though, to view these charges as a business cost, not as an added burden. For individual transactions, therefore, fees should always be factored in. Difficulty to do that will only hurt the bottom line.

Management fees: Rental properties are unique in that they usually occur over an extended period. While most approaches for leaving real estate range from one month to six, rental properties can produce cash flow as long as the property is in use. Of course, that means that for the duration it is rented out, somebody will have to manage it. That said, there remains only one question: are you going to be that person? You have to consider whether to handle the estate or to employ a property management company's services. This way, there will be expenses to consider; make sure that all of them are paid for.

Market Indicators: As perhaps the most relevant to crunch numbers, market indicators will give you a good idea of the assets to look at. Understand the average rent charged to tenants in your area and compare those numbers with what you are likely to pay on a mortgage. It's a good idea to know how much an estate in a given market can yield. I always advise that you look at developments because you'll likely have the property for a long time. Don't let the information you choose to base your entire purchase off compromise one hot season.

Financing Rental Property: Location

We've seen it all before; place, location, location. It's safe to say that position is king at this stage. For that matter, the neighborhood in which you choose to rent is just about the only thing on a property you can't change; make it count. You can even consider a location only once you have run the numbers and know how much you can invest in a rental property. But what makes a good location for a rental property?

An attractive neighborhood: it's not surprising that you want to purchase a rental property in a desirable neighborhood. While your price point may dictate where you buy, I can assure you that owning a less attractive property in a desirable neighborhood is better than a pristine property in a neighborhood in which no one wants to live. Consider this: as a rental property owner, the request will be your best friend or worst enemy. If you're having trouble finding a home in an already desirable neighborhood, try your research. Try to identify developments and forecast which location will be one of the most common communities. Go to your local municipality and see where you are planning new shopping malls or even schools. Stay ahead of the curve and find a rental property with unlimited potential for me.

Local amenities: Renters, especially Millennials, will always favor outdoor locations with amenities. That said, you should consider which amenities you are considering are located near any prospective rental property. Are there nearby any good schools? Is there public transportation in the area? Are there any areas within walking distance? All these elements, and more lead to a great location.

Financing Rental Property: Tenants

It's highly recommended that a particular type of occupant be catered. However, I would not necessarily commit to making that decision yourself; the place where you are planning to rent should dictate to whom you are most likely to rent. You will concentrate your efforts more on an idea to which you want to appeal. Remember this: there will be different needs for different types of tenants. You may want to consider turning your attention to students when you lease near a school. However, landlords may want to take advantage of the year-round weather forecasts in a place like San Diego. In other words, let the site dictate who you are renting to and how you intend to rent it.

In general, students should typically focus on location and low maintenance. Anything close to the school should get a lot of attention, but don't forget that they're going to be mostly busy with school, so they don't want to have to worry about a lot of maintenance.

On the other hand, families are more likely to favor unfurnished properties; those that they can use to represent their own home as a blank canvas. Do not hesitate, as long as it is constructive, to let families leave their own mark on a property. Families are going to want to paint, decorate, and make the house feel like home. If you allow them to do so, finding tenants will be much easier.

Financing Rental Property: Your Credit

It was best for those in search of the ideal rental property to make sure they were ready for what is in store. That said, before you even start transcending the wall between homeowners and lenders, there's one thing you have to do: test your credit score. The sooner you can come to terms with your credit score and any subsequent errors that may arise, the better it will be to search for your rental property. If for nothing else, you can fix any issues that might become possible hurdles in the future. Be proactive and take care of any credit issues before you can close with positive cash flow on a property. Consumers are entitled to a free copy of their credit report every 12 months, according to the Federal Trade Commission.

Those who are made aware of their credit history's shortcomings are encouraged not to take drastic measures, but rather to contact an expert. Someone with experience in dealing with credit issues will know the right course of action, while somebody who has no idea what they are doing might be doing more harm than good. Not unexpectedly, a lasting impact can have even small changes. Remember not to lock old accounts and pay back settlement accounts without first agreeing it would be in the best interest to do so.

Rental property funding can require a lot of due diligence on your behalf, but it can be a great career move, including a good way to grow your real estate business. In fact, in years to come, it could potentially generate passive income. Do not make the jump into a landlord, however, until you consider what's in store.

How To Apply (& Get Accepted) For Real Estate Loans

Talking about the ins and outs of real estate mortgages is the first step in purchasing your dream home.

Homebuyers usually use a real estate loan, which is also referred to as a mortgage, to fund real estate. If accepted, lenders sign a legal document (known as a mortgage note) pledging to repay the loan over some time with interest and other expenses. A property loan is generally one of the least expensive ways to finance a home, but it can also be one of the most intimidating processes undertaken by a beginner home buyer.

Even when applying for loans for real estate investment, recognizing the value of planning is important. The request (and approval) process for a mortgage loan can be both time-consuming and complicated, as it takes a tremendous amount of time, documentation, and diligence to complete. However, home buyers can do a couple of preliminary tasks to make the process smoother. Learn how to get a real estate loan today through our guide below.

What Is A Real Estate Loan

A real estate mortgage is borrowing used to buy a property, and prospective homeowners and real estate investors alike have several forms available. Each type of loan will come with different requirements for approval, interest rates, and terms. Until settling on one, it's important to explore the options available to you. Pay attention to the terms and conditions of each type of loan to ensure that you choose the correct one for your case. While real estate loans are most commonly referred to traditional mortgages, in fact there are several ways to finance a property.

Real Estate Investment Loans

A mortgage to invest in real estate refers to borrowing used to purchase an investment property rather than a primary residence. While some mortgages can not be extended to investment properties, lenders have access to a wide range of funding options. Investors may also have the flexibility to choose alternatives with higher interest rates and shorter loan terms, based on the quality of a given contract. Here are a few forms of mortgage loans for real estate to look at:

Traditional loans: banks and other lending institutions grant traditional loans or mortgages. Usually, these mortgages have acceptance requirements based on your personal financial history and often fail to take into account future rental income. Investors are also required to put down 20 percent of an estate (or charge private mortgage insurance) for conventional mortgages.

Private Money: this form of lending applies to investors supplying other investors with money. The motivation to provide a private money loan is to earn money as it is paid back with interest. This arrangement is popular among developers in real estate because the time frame for acceptance is often quicker (and sometimes more relaxed) than other funding options.

Home Equity: One option available to buyers is to take advantage of their existing home equity. This can be done through a mortgage for home equity, a credit line for home equity (HELOC), and money-out refinancing. Each of these three alternatives has slightly different conditions for acceptance and loan stipulations, but they work the same. Investors who use these types of loans may take the use of their current capital and buy another asset.

Qualifying Investment Loans: Investors who meet certain requirements or are willing to buy property in certain areas also have funding options available. Other types of loans include VA loans, USDA loans, 203k loans, etc. While not everyone has access to these options, it is certainly worth considering as they can offer some favorable terms for loans.

Hard Money Loans For Real Estate

Hard money loans in real estate are a good option for investors hoping to secure access to finance without a lengthy process of approval. Hard money loans are secured by collateral (rather than the ability of a borrower to repay) as opposed to a traditional real estate loan. This means the lender would sell the asset — in this case, a property— if the borrower were to default on loan payments. It is known that hard money loans have high-interest rates and typically last only from one to five years. They remain, however, an attractive option for real estate investors hoping to secure short-term property loans.

Crowdfunding Real Estate Loans

Crowdfunding real estate loans allow investors to finance deals from multiple potential lenders using smaller contributions. Crowdfunding purchases are usually done online and can be carried out using several platforms for social media. The attraction of a deal is that it allows real estate investors to expand their network while using a non-traditional financing option as well. Crowdfunding immovable loans can allow investors to support their companies as they advertise the popularity of the transactions.

Real Estate Bridge Loans

Bridge loans are temporary funding options that are secured by the existing property of an investor. They can be used before selling the previous property to buy a new property. This setup allows investors or home buyers to "bridge" the gap from one property to another without having to worry about selling and buying at the same time. Bridging loans, especially the fact that they can be more expensive than using other loan options, has a few drawbacks. In addition to the bridge loan, borrowers will also be responsible for payments to their existing mortgage or loan.

How To Qualify For A Real Estate Mortgage In 10 Steps

The path to home ownership starts with finance, as this will decide everything from your plan to timeframe for buying a home. Thankfully, a few steps can be taken in advance by prospective homeowners to get the process started. To know how to apply for a real estate mortgage, read through the steps below:

Check Your Credit

The first move in securing an immovable loan begins with testing the mortgage. The process includes pulling your credit report to assess where your credit score is, as this three-digit number is a necessary ingredient for a traditional lender to borrow money.

"Credit scores are a key component of the home buying cycle which influences everything from the size of a mortgage payment to the interest rate on a home loan," said TransUnion Senior Vice President Ken Chaplin. "People with subprime credit can face financial barriers to homeownership, making it difficult for their dream home to become a reality." Most credit scoring models have their appraisal process. FICO, the most common scoring model, will analyze a points credit score with a range of credit scores: bad credit (300–600), poor credit (600–649), fair credit (650–699), good credit (700–749), good credit (750–850). A credit score estimate would typically consist of five main factors:

- Payment history= 35%
- Outstanding balance= 30%
- Credit history= 15%
- Account type= 10%
- Credit inquiries= 10%

A low credit score will not automatically disqualify you from a home loan or real estate contract, but it will affect several of the loan's key factors, including size, mortgage rate, and access to certain loan programs. For homebuyers, a quality credit score is a great asset, and they can work continuously to improve it.

Perform A Credit Audit

Once you have taken your credit report and checked your credit score, now is the time to run a credit check. In essence, this process takes a highlight to your credit report to outline what you have done right, where you have gone wrong, and how you can improve. This move is commonly performed in the early stages of applying for a home loan, as the necessary adjustments can sometimes take weeks, months, and even years.

Dispute Inaccuracies, Early Fees & False Data

Now is the credit report's time to counter inaccuracies. Since negative information can adversely affect your chances of securing an immovable loan, it is critical that homebuyers not only review their credit report but also examine and verify that everything is correct.

It is advised that homebuyers wishing to refute inaccuracies contact both the credit office and the company providing the office with the data. Two agencies are responsible for correcting incorrect or incomplete information on your credit report under the Equal Credit Reporting Act. This can be done in two steps in most cases:

- Step One: Call the credit manager and let them know what you think is wrong. This should include identifying each item in your credit report that you dispute, explaining why you dispute the information, and a request for correction, as well as providing your full name and address. This should also include copies of any information related to your dispute.
- Step Two: Call the relevant lenders to clarify to them that you are contesting the information provided to the agency. This also involves submitting copies of your work supporting documents.

Pay Off Debt

Debt-to-income is another factor to secure a real estate mortgage. To decide how much you can fairly pay, creditors will compare how much you earn with how much you invest. In most cases, lenders will not approve a home buyer if their debt exceeds 36% of their income, with some lenders requiring higher debt-to-income ratios. The two types of debt-to-income ratios that lenders are generally looking for are:

- Front-end ratio: this applies to the cost of housing, including the percentage of income to be charged.
- Back-end figure: this calculation measures how much a prospective homebuyer owes liabilities, such as credit card bills, car payments, child support, student loans and other obligations.

The best thing that a home buyer can do when planning to apply for a real estate mortgage is to reduce the amount of money they owe. Reducing credit card balances or other financial obligations will help lower the percentage of your income to pay monthly debt. This will ultimately help free up cash, including how much money you can borrow.

Determine What You Can Afford

In the beginning stages, a common mistake home buyers make is to look for the home they want, rather than what they can afford comfortably. While lenders will have lending guidelines in place to determine how much money you can borrow, it is also important for you and your family to make financial sense to buy a house. That said, when starting, it is imperative for potential homebuyers to consider both their current (and future) finances. Renting may be a better option than buying in some cases, so it is important to compare the cost of renting vs. buying to gain a better understanding of where you are.

Gather Work History

Another important factor in obtaining a real estate loan is the collection of Work History Employment history. In general, lenders will want home buyers with a company to have at least two years of history, but this is not absolute. Several factors will be taken into account by lenders, including whether you were in school, military service, or career switches.

The purpose of collecting a history of work is to verify that you have a reliable source of coming money. In essence, lenders determine your level of risk, including whether or not you can make your monthly payments

Assemble Income Information

Similar to the past of employment, the profit is checked by another element to secure a real estate mortgage. Home buyers should collect their income information to verify their source of income, including pay stubs, tax returns, bank statements, brokerage statements, work contracts, and other documentation. This step is crucial not only to determine how much you can afford but also to confirm that your monthly payments can be made.

Down Payment

The next step to apply for a property loan is the down payment. The amount a homebuyer pays depends on a combination of factors, including credit and financing, — somewhere between three percent and 20 percent of the home's price. Another thing that borrowers look at is the loan-to-value ratio (LTV). This equation, which contrasts the home value with the loan value, is used by borrowers to determine the amount of uncovered risk they take on with the mortgage. A poor LTV rate, for instance, will create higher interest payments every month because you have less equity investment in your house.

In addition to the down payment, homebuyers will also need additional funds to pay in the home buying process for closing costs and other obligations. In addition, it is important for potential homebuyers to avoid opening up any new lines of credit during this process, as this may affect your chances of approval.

Compare Lenders

In securing a real estate loan, the second-to-final step is to compare your options. Whether this involves researching lenders or asking friends and family, you must take the time to examine your choices, as each lender will handle various types of loans. Remember, not all lenders offer the same loans, so it is important for homeowners to be careful when buying a home, especially when finding a lender.

Get Pre-approved, Not Pre-Qualified

The final step in securing an immovable loan is to get pre-approved. This process differs from pre-qualifying, which does not require your financial information to be accessible. Getting pre-approved lenders will allow you to run your credit and review your finances. Future home buyers are important to understand the difference between pre-approval and pre-qualified, as you will provide a much more accurate estimate of your future loan amount. You will increase your chances of securing your dream home (or investment property) by taking the time to visit creditors and update your finances.

Summary

It is not an easy task to secure real estate loans. Providing yourself with the requisite information and knowledge, as well as organizing your paperwork in advance, will serve to assist prospective homebuyers. Pay attention to the various options available to you and follow the above steps. If it sounds overwhelming right now, don't worry: any contract you land will make the process smoother.

Getting Ready To Close

Much as you had to take certain precautions when you bought your rental property when you want to sell your rental property, you also have to make some arrangements. Getting ready for yourself and your estate would help give you the best opportunities to easily market your assets for the top dollar. Before you put your property on the market, here are the steps you should take.

Paperwork

Revenue and Expense Report: Once you lease your rental property, you want to make sure you have all of your financial information in order. Preparing a profit and cost statement will provide a better picture of the value of your property for you and any potential buyer.

Income: Included in this document on income and expenses, you will want to track on a monthly or annual basis all revenue earned by the estate. This could include monthly rental payments from tenants, as well as any additional parking space rent, use of washer and dryers, or payments if you are lucky enough to have a billboard or cell phone tower on your property.

Expenses: You must also include the money you spend for the year in the income and expense report. This could include:

- Fees on land
- Claims on insurance
- Water and sewer charges: if you are paying for infrastructure.
- Fees for electricity: if you have an infrastructure.
- Fuel charges: if you have electricity.
- Oil charges: if you are in charge of utilities.
- Maintenance: an amount of maintenance is calculated by most stakeholders or Realtors. This amount is traditionally 5% of gross operating income. The cost of maintenance can vary depending on the size of the estate, the age of the property and the amount of outside storage. It can include items like cost of landscaping, expense of restoring and removing outdated and failed fixtures, door locks, walls, broken doors, plumbing leakage, roof leaks, and wobbly railings.

Gather Reports Related to Taxes, Expenses, and Property Management

Items from Revenue and Expense Report: You will want to find hard copies of the items you have included in the Revenue and Expense Report before you put the rental property up for sale. You're going to want to collect these last year's statements. All utility bills, insurance statements, property taxes, mortgage payments, rental payments, maintenance costs and so on can be included.

You should scan all these receipts into your computer to get a digital copy of them as well. This will make it easier if requested to send an item to a prospective buyer, an attorney, or a Realtor as you will have it available electronically already.

Copies of all applicable leases: for current tenants, you will want to collect copies of all lease agreements. This will be used to check the current rent payment and the length of the rent.

List of any recent improvements to the property: a list of any improvements that you have made to the property in recent years should be compiled. Have you been putting on a new roof, repairing the boiler, and renovating the kitchen, for example? You will also want to include the estimated job date and probably the approximate change cost.

You'll want to apply concise adjectives to your list of changes. For example, instead of saying, refurbished kitchen, it might be more appealing to say, refurbished kitchen, including gray shaker cabinets, polar white granite, and beveled subway backsplash.

Otherwise, you must find any evidence of the work that has been done. Copies of invoices, work contracts, or other documents could be this.

The Realtor will often use a list of improvements when preparing the property listing information. This list should, therefore, be as thorough as possible.

Copies of any licenses: the first thing you need to do is to ensure that your land does not have available permits. You can make this request in person, on the phone or online, depending on your city. This is referred to as a request for open public records.

If the property has any open permits, you'll probably have to close them out before selling. You will need to determine what work needs to be done, hire a licensed contractor to complete the work, then get a city inspector to come out and check that the work has been done to code so that they can close the license.

For any work that has ever been completed on the property, you should collect or obtain copies of all permits. The municipality should be able to provide you with copies of all approved land permits.

Determine Profit Potential

To get an estimate of how much cash you can make if you sell your house, you can assess your finances.

- How much of your mortgage, do you owe? Do you have any penalties for advance payment?
- Know the closing costs during the sale of your property that you will be responsible for. This could include real estate transfer tax on the purchase, realtor commission on selling, registration fees, and payment for the lawyer.
- Know your tax base for the property, so you know how much you owe in taxes. Consult with your auditor to assess your tax base.
- Know what your property's rough market value is. You can consider two or three similar properties that have been sold in the last year in your city. Such figures can be used to get a rough idea of the price range the estate should be sold in.
- Use your property's approximate market value, minus the amount you owe on your mortgage, minus closing costs for selling your home to decide how much cash you'd walk away with on sale.
- Then you have to calculate how much money you owe for taxes on capital gains. To do this, you'll use the property's selling price less the tax base you've estimated. That number will decide what you have to pay for taxes on capital gains. Make sure you talk to your auditor because

there may be cases where you walk away with very little cash on sale, but owe much more in taxes on capital gains due to write-offs made throughout the property's possession.

Maintenance

Deferred Maintenance: You want your estate to look as good as possible before the auction. This is the time to address any maintenance problems that you have delayed. This may include lighting common areas, enhancing the appearance of landscaping and curbing, replacing running toilets, and small drips in faucets.

Capital Improvements: You must also determine whether it is worthwhile to complete any capital improvements before the sale. Is the investment going to yield a greater return than it costs? Could you put a new roof on the house for less than the market rate, for example?

Would spending more money in the estate makes sense? If you don't make improvements like this, will it minimize the sales possibility? Will a poor roof, decaying deck or wall holes dissuade anyone from buying the property?

General Tips

Notify tenants: If your rental property is on the market, prospective buyers will need to be able to enter at least one rental unit while visiting the house. Therefore, you would have to decide whether and how to tell tenants that you are selling the property. You may not have to notify all tenants of your intention to sell the property, depending on the size of your property. Only the residents whose units you want to present prospective buyers will need to be told.

When they hear that the property is going up for sale, sometimes tenants are afraid. We fear when it's sold, they'll be displaced. They also worry about how the property will be managed by a new landlord. Some tenants will also use this as an opportunity for reasonable and unreasonable issues to wind up against the landlord, so be careful to allow tenants to interact with prospective buyers.

Fill any vacancies: ideally, you will have 100% occupancy on your property before you sell. Do not cut corners to try and fill the vacancy quickly if you have a vacancy. Make sure that you continue to follow your entire screening process.

If your estate doesn't sell quickly, you'll be tied to the property with whatever occupant you put. You also don't want to put trouble tenants in the property at a moment when they need to look their best. Finding an empty unit is better than having it shared with a bad tenant.

Interview Realtors: To list your rental property, you'll need to find a Realtor. If you've already been working with a Realtor in the past and feel comfortable with it, then you're all set.

Otherwise, many Realtors will need to be consulted. Looking for Realtors who are specialized in the type of property and the area you are selling in is important. Single-family homes or condos may not need such a specialized person, but for a multi-family property, a retail property, a mixed-use property, or other more unique investments, you want to find someone who is successful in selling the type of property you are trying to sell. Think of it in the same way that attorneys are trained in certain fields such as divorce, business, and corporate law.

When to Put It on the Market

Investment properties do not follow the same rules as the sale to homeowners of primary residences. The normal housing market is strongest in the spring, as before the new school year, families are trying to enter their new homes.

Generally speaking, you can sell an investment property at any time of the year. You can see less activity during the holidays or summer.

Close With Confidence!

You will be able to move into your new home once you nail down these steps! Contact a professional if you need further insight into any of these aspects.

Conclusion

Investing in real estate, particularly on your first time out, can be an overwhelming experience. To get all the money you may need to get started investing in real estate can be a daunting task. But you don't have to try to do it alone. A Real Estate Investment Club is a great way to bring people with different skills and strengths together to function as a single investment group.

There are various types of equity partners that give any asset that is beneficial to the rest of the members individually to the community. You may have construction experience or even a contractor, but you lack the knowledge you need to find or locate properties or other things. Maybe you need to get started with the money. If the latter is valid, this dimension of the problem can be solved by having a cash partner. You can have a great source of property leads by bringing in a licensed real estate agent to be a member. Likewise, you can benefit from his or her knowledge of the finance industry by finding a person who works in finance.

The real estate market is very volatile, and holding a property for a very long time is not a good idea unless you have enough money to cope with temporary losses. The best choice would be to keep an eye on the market or place the property for sale when the properties start to be sold in any particular area as hot bread.

You also need to keep an eye on the market when it comes to buying properties, but mainly to see when selling a property is a good offer. The thing is that you need a fair amount of money to buy and hold on until the market recovers when everybody sells. But you can make great deals without waiting so much with special offers due to personal reasons (a personal need to sell).

www.ingramcontent.com/pod-product-compliance
Lightning Source LLC
Chambersburg PA
CBHW070648220526
45466CB00001B/345